BOSS SIMON

Joseph Simon: The First Jewish Republican Senator

RICHARD SIMON

Introduction

Political devil. The Judas Iscariot of Oregon politics. Little Napoleon. Senatorial Prevaricator. Joe the Big Boss.

Those were among the terms used to describe Joseph Simon, the nation's first Jewish Republican U.S. senator.

Simon served as a Portland mayor, city councilman and police commissioner, five-time president of the Oregon state Senate and chairman of the state Republican Party. He was a member of one of the West's most prestigious law firms, representing powerful railroads.

And he was a political boss.

He hobnobbed with U.S. presidents. But he had an ugly falling out with Teddy Roosevelt, accusing the president of discriminating against him because he was Jewish.

I heard about my famous relative from my father. But no one in the family knew much about Senator Simon. So, I decided to look into his life.

Imagine my surprise when I found him described as ``worse than a Southern Pacific train robber.''

And, a man ``who would not hesitate to use any means short of committing an actual felony to gain a political end.'' But hey, he was never indicted.

I also discovered an immigrant success story: a German-born Jew who never finished high school but became a prominent lawyer and one of the most influential—and controversial—politicians in Oregon. ``He is one of Oregon's self-made men,'' the Los Angeles Times marveled.

His election to the U.S. Senate was ``one of the greatest political surprises ever,'' as one newspaper put it.

It came after Simon and his allies shut down the state Capitol for an entire legislative session in a political drama worthy of ``House of Cards.''

A strange-bedfellows alliance entertained lawmakers (probably with generous libations and amiable companionship) to keep them away from the statehouse and prevent the election of a Simon rival to the U.S. Senate. At the time, state legislators chose U.S. senators.

Simon won the U.S. Senate seat. But public outrage over his and his supporters' obstructionist tactics—the Legislature failed to pass a single law during the entire session—contributed to the drive for a Constitutional amendment providing for the election of U.S. senators by a vote of the people.

Simon's wheeling and dealing lent momentum to other political reforms, including Oregon's game-changing initiative and referendum, which became a model for other states. The initiative process has produced thousands of voter-approved laws across the country, from creating state lotteries to establishing term limits for elected officials.

``Oregon has undergone a silent revolution against Simonism,'' the Portland Municipal Association said. A number of Oregon political reforms were a ``protest against the condition for which Joseph Simon, as much or more than any other man, was responsible,'' the group wrote the Oregon Journal.

While condemned as a ``schemer,'' ``scurvy villain,'' and ``blight upon the name of Oregon,'' Joe Simon dedicated his life to public service and worked tirelessly to promote Portland as the leading city in the Pacific Northwest.

``Among the noteworthy events that I have observed,'' he said at a 1922 luncheon to honor his 50 years as a lawyer, ``was the coming of the Union Pacific to Oregon. I was active in getting through the legislation that permitted the great railroad to establish itself here.''

His work to expand the railroad, promote commerce and develop Portland's water system were critical to the region's growth.

Simon was known as the ``Little Napoleon of the Republican Party of Oregon,'' though, at 5-foot-5, he was shorter than the 5-foot-6 emperor.

Yet, he loomed large in the rough-and-tumble world of politics in the late 19th and early 20th centuries.

``There is not in the political history of the state of Oregon a more unique and interesting figure than that of the Hon. Joseph Simon," The Pacific Monthly wrote after Simon's election to the U.S. Senate in 1898.

``Perhaps no one man, since the territory of Oregon was admitted to statehood, has exercised so strong an influence, has played so important a part, or has shown so masterful a hand in shaping the political destinies of this quiet and conservative corner of the world," the magazine added.

In addition to being the first Jewish Republican senator, he was the first Jewish senator of any party from the West.

If Senator Simon were alive, I doubt he would have talked to me for this write up.

He hated newspapermen.

Perhaps it was because he was ``the object of more newspaper criticism and abuse than any other politician in the state," as the Corvallis Gazette noted.

His wariness was understandable. The newspapers of his era were fiercely partisan.

Simon overcame adversity.

He thought he had won a razor-thin mayor's race only to lose it after an acrimonious recount. He came back and won the job more than 25 years later. Oregon's political leadership recommended him for a coveted federal judgeship. (Some of Simon's critics liked the idea of him leaving Oregon politics and moving out of state if he landed the job.) But he failed to win the presidential appointment. Still, Simon went on to snag a prestigious U.S. Senate seat.

He also survived an assault during a tumultuous Republican convention.

Simon witnessed historic events. He was in Oregon Territory when it became the 33rd state. He served in the Senate when a fistfight broke out in the ``world's most deliberative body." He was on hand to welcome Rutherford B. Hayes to Oregon when he became the first sitting president to travel west of the Rockies. Simon also was present for the driving of last spikes to mark completion of railroad segments that drove settlement of the West.

As a U.S. senator, Simon cast votes on landmark legislation, including a bill paving the way for building the Panama Canal. He voted for the treaty ending the Spanish-American War, an irrigation bill that was critical to the development of the West, a pure food law and a measure providing pensions for veterans of Indian wars. He flashed a thumbs up for the first federal wildlife protection law and legislation to preserve hundreds of California's majestic giant sequoia trees.

He made his biggest splash on the national stage by suggesting that Theodore Roosevelt treated him poorly because he was Jewish.

``Simon Scores the President for Discriminating Against Him Because He Is a Jew," read the headline in the Daily Picayune in New Orleans.

The charge enraged Roosevelt. Yet, the two men greeted each other warmly years later when the former president visited Portland.

A look at Simon's life shows how much some things have changed and how much some haven't since his times.

Among the issues he faced: a bill allowing voters to decide, ``Shall swine be allowed to run at large?"

The temperance movement was big during his days. Another hot issue, believe it or not, was prizefighting.

Simon was at the center of debates over immigration, trade, regulation of corporate behavior, federal spending and America's role in the world, all issues that are still hotly debated.

The U.S. Senate during his time was, as the New Orleans Times-Picayune put it, a ``tornado of partisan debate." Sound familiar?

Today, Simon is little remembered, even in his hometown.

No statue of him stands in the city he cherished. No street is named after him. A World War II Liberty ship, the Joseph Simon, was sold for scrap long ago. A painting of him that once hung in City Hall is at the Oregon Historical Society – in storage.

Hardly a fitting tribute for a man described as ``the most notorious boss Oregon has ever known."

Joe Simon's life story is a portrait of an immigrant's fulfillment of the American dream.

``That he is and has been a 'boss' is true; that at times he has been the most abused and hated by even his own party is also true; that he is a partisan of partisans is also true, but that he is a man of brains, a tireless worker, a man who succeeded is also true," wrote the Prineville Review of Oregon.

Joseph Simon. Courtesy of the Oregon Historical
Society, Oregonian collection.

Simon's life story also is a tale of the bare-knuckle politics of party bosses that led to newspaper stories of ``boodle turned loose,'' dirty tricks, vote buying, ballot stuffing and Simon ward heelers reaching into ``dives'' to recruit voters, whether they were eligible to vote, or sober.

Simon did not fit the image of a political boss.

The mustachioed master of machine politics was soft spoken, polite and kept a low profile. He didn't drink, smoke or swear. He was, the Medford, Ore., Mail wrote, a ``gentleman of kindly instincts and genuine good fellowship.''

He was a humble man, ``not given to hot-air methods of blowing his own horn,'' the Capital Journal in Salem wrote.

When Simon ran for mayor, he pledged, ``I shall not resort to the use of brass bands or anything spectacular in an effort to promote my election,'' the Oregonian reported.

As mayor of Portland, Simon took on what his predecessor described as the toughest job in Oregon with ``more kind of hell in it than Dante ever imagined." On taking office, Simon found himself in a political inferno, coming under heavy pressure to suppress the city's "social evil."

He was a man of contradictions.

While he was a teetotaler who sought to cut the number of saloons in Portland from 418 to 100, Simon championed Oregon's beer industry. He spoke out against Prohibition. And he represented famed brewer Henry Weinhard in a court challenge to alcohol restrictions.

While he was attacked as cozy with Big Business, he supported some of President Theodore Roosevelt's trust-busting legislation, including regulation of his railroad industry friends.

He was an immigrant who achieved the American dream. Yet, he joined the shameful stampede to exclude Chinese immigrants from the United States.

While he supported the building of a museum to showcase women's contributions, he voted against giving women the right to vote.

He drew praise as a man of principle for defying party leaders on a number of Senate votes. Yet, when he opposed the election of a fellow Republican for Oregon chief justice, he was branded a traitor to his party.

While Simon was mild-mannered, his machine could play rough. Consider this headline in the Seattle Post-Intelligencer: "Joseph Simon Wins. Turbulent Scenes at the Portland Republican Primaries. One Man Loses An Ear."

In perhaps the most stunning contradiction of his career, Boss Simon, in one of his last official acts, championed a political reform: creation of Portland's unusual commission form of government.

As he neared the end of his political career, the Boss even drew praise from a good government group.

"Whatever you say, Simon was never himself a grafter," said Clinton Rogers Woodruff of the National Municipal League.

Simon, a lifelong bachelor, wasn't all business. He enjoyed riding around in that newfangled contraption: the automobile. He also played the banjo.

He built a fortune for himself as an investor in railroads, coal mines, steamboats, real estate, banking, a sawmill—and a candy company.

He had a soft spot for the less fortunate. Simon loaned his car out for children to see what it was like to ride in an automobile. And, he provided free legal services to community groups.

Although best known for being a railroad lawyer, Simon's legal work ran the gamut, from divorce to murder cases.

He defended a man accused of smuggling opium and Chinese laborers into the United States. He represented a congressman charged with corruption. And he pushed for the pardon of a convicted killer who made headlines by becoming a judge after his release from prison.

Simon rose to power during the Gilded Age and, like other political bosses, saw his clout diminish under Progressive Era reforms. He lived during a period of dramatic change, from the stagecoach era to the dawn of the aviation age.

He endured tough times, including a devastating Portland fire in 1873, the great gale of 1880, the Panic of 1893, Portland's Great Flood of 1894 and the Great Blizzard of 1899.

During his lifetime, Simon saw headlines like "A Bloody Battle in the Streets of Tombstone" (referring to the gunfight at O.K. Corral); "Earthquake and Fire: San Francisco In Ruins;" "Commander Peary Reaches North Pole;" "Machine Flies Like a Huge Bird" (the Wright Brothers' flight); "Don't Let the Comet Scare You!" (the passing of Halley's Comet); and "Titanic Loss Greatest of All Disasters."

And there were these, too: "Proof of Life on Planet Mars" and "Martians Finish Canal On Planet," in reference to an astronomer's 1910 discovery of a new canal on the red planet, "proof that the planet Mars is inhabited."

Simon crossed paths with colorful figures, perhaps none more than Republican Sen. John Mitchell, a bigamist, adulterer and thief who lived under an assumed name to hide his misdeeds.

And yet, Mitchell was one of Oregon's most popular politicians.

He also was Simon's bitter enemy.

CHAPTER ONE
An Oregon pioneer

Joseph Simon was born Feb. 7, 1851 in Bechtheim, a small village in the Grand Duchy of Hesse-Darmstadt west of the Rhine. Today, the area is part of Germany.

Joe was a year old when his parents David and Elise (Leopold) Simon emigrated to the United States, most likely to flee religious persecution and political turmoil.

The family entered the country through New Orleans and moved to Sacramento and then San Francisco.

The Simons arrived in Oregon Territory in the fall of 1857, two years before Oregon became the 33rd state.

``The settlement of Oregon coincided with a high tide of German immigration to America, and many of the first Jewish Oregonians were of German origin,'' Ralph Friedman wrote in ``The Jews of Oregon'' in a 1954 issue of the Brooklyn Jewish Center Review.

``The early Jews were, like the other settlers, pioneers in the real sense,'' he added.

What brought the Simons to Oregon is unknown, but it could have been the economic opportunities created by gold strikes in California and Oregon.

Joseph was the oldest of four children. Other family members were Samuel (who became a partner in the prominent Portland mercantile firm of Fleischner, Mayer & Co.), Nathan (an attorney) and Minnie Oberdorfer.

When the family arrived—probably by steamboat and stagecoach— Portland was still a frontier town with fewer than 3,000 residents.

``Jewish pioneers appeared in Portland almost at the point of the city's founding—a circumstance which served to aid their integration and acceptance into the frontier community," Robert Scott Cline wrote in "Community Structure on the Urban Frontier: the Jews of Portland, Oregon, 1849-1887."

Joseph's father David was among eight men who attended a meeting to plan for the Pacific Northwest's first synagogue, Beth Israel, in 1858. At the time, there were only about 30 Jewish families in Portland.

The first services were held in a loft above a stable. The congregation moved into its first synagogue in 1861. Joe later served as a trustee and vice president of the temple board.

Joe, at age 8, was likely on hand on March 15, 1859 when a steamer arrived in Portland from San Francisco carrying the news of Oregon statehood.

It took a month for word to reach the city after President Buchanan signed the statehood bill. The news was transmitted by telegraph to St. Louis, stagecoach to San Francisco and steamer to Portland.

Portland wouldn't have a telegraph connection to the East until 1864. When the line was completed, the city broke out "in a blaze of glory," newspapers reported. A torchlight procession was held in front of the telegraph office. One of the first messages sent from Portland was addressed to President Lincoln.

"Our telegraph is complete." Oregon Gov. Addison Gibbs wired to Lincoln. "Let the great Pacific Railroad with a branch to Oregon soon follow. We want no Pacific Republic. No compromise with rebels in arms. No more slavery."

In 1865, when Lee surrendered to Grant at Appomattox, Joe was 14 years old.

News of the end of the Civil War touched off "the greatest celebration that Portland had ever seen," as the Oregonian put it. But the jubilation was short lived.

A few days later, the Portland telegraph office received a short message: "Lincoln assassinated."

Joe was likely on hand when Portland mourned the president's death.

Joe attended a school run by Sylvester Pennoyer, who became an Oregon governor and recommended his former pupil for a federal judgeship but clashed with him on legislation.

At age 14, Joe left school to work in his father's general merchandise store.

``My father started his store in Portland while Oregon was still a territory,'' he recalled in a 1922 interview with the Oregon Journal.

``We sold whatever the people would buy, and we bought whatever they offered—butter, bacon, eggs, and other produce of all kinds. In the early days, trade here in Portland was largely a matter of barter, as there were fewer wage earners and more actual producers.''

Joe, at age 19, left the store and began studying law in the office of John H. Mitchell and Joseph N. Dolph, the state's leading railroad law firm.

Two years later, he was admitted to the bar.

He then lost his first case.

The case was tried before Barney Trainer, an East Portland justice of the peace who ran a saloon.

The judge decided that ``inasmuch as the defendant of the case is a widow woman, and moreover as she lives here in East Portland, I'll decide the case in her favor,'' Simon recalled for the Oregon Journal.

Losing the case didn't hurt Simon's career. In 1873, he became a partner in the firm.

After Mitchell was elected to the Senate, the firm became Dolph, Bronaugh, Dolph & Simon. It underwent more name changes as partners changed.

``For many years, this law firm was virtually the governmental headquarters of the state – managed Republican politics, ruled the state Legislature and made and unmade United States senators,'' Burton J. Hendrick wrote in McClure's Magazine in 1911. The Republican State Central Committee often met in the firm's offices.

The firm—key to Simon's rise in business and political circles—produced four U.S. senators: Joseph N. Dolph, John Hipple Mitchell, John M. Gearin and Simon. Its members included an ex-congressman, former Oregon chief justice and future federal judge.

``Simon became a leading corporate lawyer during the next decade and developed a political power base that made him the most powerful Republican in the state,'' Cline wrote.

``There is no better known lawyer in the state than Senator Joseph

Simon," H. James Boswell wrote in the 1921 book, "The Blue Book of Portland and Adjacent Cities."

Simon and Mitchell, though both Republicans, became bitter enemies and leaders of rival factions within the party.

Their loathing for each other was compared to the bad blood between the Montagues and Capulets in Romeo and Juliet.

Mitchell was among the most colorful characters in Oregon history.

While a 26-year-old teacher in Pennsylvania, John Mitchell Hipple (his real name) seduced a 15-year-old student. He married her after she became pregnant.

He then abandoned his family for his mistress. Hipple, who had become a lawyer, also absconded with clients' money.

He left his mistress to marry a different woman—without divorcing his first wife—and carried on an affair with his second wife's younger sister. After moving West, he changed his name to John H. Mitchell.

Even after his indiscretions became public, with the Oregonian publishing his love letters to his second wife's sister, Mitchell was reelected to the U.S. Senate.

The Oregon Republican Party passed a resolution in 1873 declaring that whatever Mitchell's "misfortunes, faults or shortcomings" were early in his private life, he had redeemed himself through his work on behalf of the state. The public seemed to agree.

After Simon and his allies engineered Mitchell's ouster from the U.S. Senate, Mitchell mounted a remarkable comeback.

Incredibly, the two men ended up serving together in the Senate.

But their relationship was so toxic that when Oregon's senators were invited to the White House, they went separately.

(Friction between senators from the same state and same party is more common than thought; the Senate, after all, has been called "an institution with 100 large egos and 200 sharp elbows." During Simon's time in the chamber, South Carolina's Democratic senators got into a fistfight. In the late 1990s, New Jersey's then Democratic senators refused to speak to each other for nearly a year.)

Senator John H. Mitchell. Courtesy of the Brady-Handy photograph collection, Library of Congress, Prints and Photographs Division.

While Simon and Mitchell were Republicans, they chose to form coalitions with Democrats to try to gain the upper hand over each other.

Mitchell later became one of the few U.S. senators convicted of a crime while in office. He died while appealing his conviction.

Even after his legal troubles, thousands turned out at Portland City Hall where Mitchell's body laid in state.

``Mitchell was popular with the people,'' the Medford Tribune wrote. ``Simon was a great wire puller, strong with politicians, but unpopular with the masses.''

Mitchell had a ``charming personality and was an effective and engaging public speaker,'' the Statesman Journal wrote.

He was a skilled politician, too.

He once used a 60-pound salmon to score a political victory.

It was 1902. Mitchell was seeking to establish an assay office in Portland.

``He could not get the Senate interested in it at all,'' the Los Angeles Times reported.

During a Senate debate, Mitchell told colleagues that he had received the fish and would like to share it.

Senators recessed to the Senate restaurant. After lunch, Mitchell brought up his bill, and this time, the Senate bit—hook, line and sinker. It approved the assay office.

Mitchell also secured a big appropriation for Portland's Lewis and Clark Exposition by staging a splashy dinner for fellow lawmakers.

``The way to a man's vote is through his stomach,'' a fellow lawmaker quipped.

In contrast, Simon was a cautious, private man who preferred writing letters and reading reports to attending social events.

He was not one for stemwinders. He was called the silent man of the Senate, delivering only one memorable speech during his days under the Capitol dome.

Yet, Simon was praised for his straightforward manner and independent streaks. A behind-the-scenes operator, he was described by the Oregon Journal as ``the shrewdest political organizer who ever played the game of Oregon politics.''

Simon's political activities came at a time when Oregon – now a blue state – was solidly Republican.

Many Jews became Republicans because they ``strongly opposed slavery, and supported Lincoln—to whom Jews felt particularly drawn by his character, self-deprecating humor and sense of humanity,'' Steven Lowenstein wrote in ``The Jews of Oregon.''

At synagogues, Lincoln was compared to Moses.

Simon became politically well-connected through his firm's legal work for the powerful railroads, his leadership positions in the Republican Party and his association with his influential law partners and Portland businessmen.

His legal work, political activities and business ties also helped him become wealthy.

In 1900, Simon appeared on a New York World list of millionaire U.S.

senators. (A saying of the times was: ``It is harder for a poor man to enter the United States Senate than for a rich man to enter Heaven.'')

Among his law firm's clients was legendary railroad king Henry Villard, who brought the transcontinental railroad to Oregon in 1883.

Villard was one of the most interesting characters Simon met.

A German immigrant, he worked as a newspaperman, covering the Lincoln-Douglas debates and Civil War battles. An early backer of inventor Thomas Edison, he became a big promoter of electricity and founding president of Edison General Electric Company.

Villard, through his work in building the transcontinental railroad and promoting the Pacific Northwest, gave Simon a front row seat to historic events and an opportunity to meet movers and shakers.

Simon may have been in attendance in Montana Territory—along with former President Ulysses S. Grant, members of President Chester A. Arthur's Cabinet, six governors, foreign dignitaries and more than 3,000 others—-for driving of the last spike to mark completion of the Northern Pacific Railroad.

Guests included West Coast VIPs brought in from Portland on trains decked out in red, white and blue. "Last Spike Specials" brought business and government leaders from the East by train, along with barons, counts, earls, lords and other foreign dignitaries.

Railroad president Villard, who hosted the Sept. 8, 1883 celebration about 60 miles west of Helena, sought to put on a good show, especially for prospective investors. One newspaper described it as an ``extraordinary spectacle.''

An ornately decorated pavilion was built for seating of the guests, ``many of them distinguished gentlemen, eminent in the eyes of the world for their learning, character, titles or money,'' wrote the New North-West, a Montana newspaper. A military band played. A horse that had hauled rail for the railroad was brought on stage, and, according to news reports, received an ovation.

``Three hundred men with brawny arms quickly laid the iron and drove the spikes on the 1,000 feet of uncompleted track, except the last spike,'' a Chicago Tribune correspondent wrote. The last spike was hammered in by a railroad official who drove the first spike 13 years earlier. Telegraph wires were set up so that news of the railroad's completion was flashed coast to coast as the spike maul struck. As the final spike was pounded, bells rang in Portland.

The Columbian newspaper of St. Helens, Ore. called the line's completion "one of the grandest events of American history," trumpeting: "You can go from Portland, Oregon to St. Paul, Minnesota in 97 hours."

Simon was on hand a few days later, along with just about all of Portland, for the arrival of the first through train from the East.

The Sept. 11, 1883 celebration was described by the Oregonian as "the grandest sight that Portland had ever witnessed."

An enthusiastic crowd welcomed the railroad's completion with elaborate decorations, a long parade, a military band, songs from 300 schoolchildren, an evening concert, and, of course, speeches. Virtually all businesses were shut down for the day.

The parade included soldiers, Oregon pioneers and wagons featuring coal, lumber, wool, sacks of flour and other local products to showcase Portland's industries.

The rolling exhibits rivaled the Rose Parade floats of today in creativity; they included a blacksmith at work over a forge, blocks of ice, with flowers and fish frozen inside, a woodman chopping a tree, and, perhaps the most popular, an "immense beer cask." Cigar manufacturers handed out stogies to the crowd.

"It was a wonderful event," Simon recalled in a 1926 interview with the Oregonian. "The people of Portland went wild, for the coming of the great Northern Pacific meant new prosperity for Portland and the Pacific Northwest."

The importance of the railroads to life in the West cannot be overstated.

The railroads opened new markets for Oregon goods and brought in settlers. They also wielded enormous political clout.

"By the end of the 1880s, the most influential lawyers and politicians—including John H. Mitchell, Cyrus Dolph, and Joseph Simon—were as notorious for their allegiance to specific railroad interests as for their political affiliation," William Toll wrote for the Oregon History Project.

Simon served as board secretary of the Oregon and Transcontinental Co., a holding company established by Villard to control the Oregon Railway and Navigation Co. and Northern Pacific Railroad Co.

So far-reaching were the company's endeavors that it boasted in its 1883 annual report of operating in a territory representing one-sixth of the area of the United States.

Yet, Villard and his railroad ran into money trouble. Only months after the last-spike ceremony, Villard was out as the Northern Pacific Railroad president.

Villard, in his memoirs ``The Early History of Transportation in Oregon,'' referred to the diligence of Simon and his law partners. On his first trip to Portland, Villard wrote, ``I had to sign my name no less than two hundred and forty times.''

Oregon and Transcontinental Co. stock certificate, signed by corporate secretary Joseph Simon, 1882. Courtesy of Special Collections, Norris L Brookens Library, University of Illinois at Springfield.

Simon was an officer and large stockholder in the Northern Pacific Terminal Co. at a time when it was Portland's second largest corporate property holder. The company opened Portland's Grand Central passenger station in 1896. The depot, renamed Union Station, is still in use.

Simon likely rubbed shoulders with some of the most prominent railroad men in U.S. history.

In his work for Villard, he could have met powerful banker J. Pierpont

Morgan, who provided critical financing to complete the transcontinental line.

Simon probably met California Senator Leland Stanford and Charles Crocker when the railroad moguls visited Portland in 1887.

Simon was likely among California and Oregon leaders in attendance later in the year for Crocker's driving of the last spike in Ashland, Ore., to mark completion of a direct rail link between Portland and San Francisco. Bells rang, cannons fired, and whistles blew in communities throughout California and Oregon when the last spike was struck.

Simon was a board member of another Villard-affiliated enterprise, the Oregon Improvement Company. (Among his fellow directors was Albert S. Rosenbaum, a German Jewish immigrant—and my great-great-grandfather—who built a fortune in the tobacco business and lived in New York.)

The company owned coal mines and railroads in Washington Territory and operated the Pacific Coast Railway in California. Its Pacific Coast Steamship Co. ran ships from San Diego to Alaska. It also operated wharves in Seattle and San Francisco and owned timber land in Oregon and Washington Territory.

Simon also was an incorporator and board secretary of the Union Pacific-backed Oregon Railway Extensions Co., which built railroads in Oregon, Washington state, Idaho and Montana.

While Simon's business interests made him wealthy, his investments could be troublesome.

The Oregon Improvement Company faced labor unrest. Its use of low-paid Chinese miners led to violence. In one attack, a building occupied by Chinese workers at a company mine near Seattle was set on fire by about a dozen masked—and armed—men.

Adding to the company's woes, some of its steamers were lost at sea. The company's mining operations also suffered from competition from cheap foreign imports.

In 1890, Simon was named receiver of the Oregon Improvement Company after it ran into money troubles.

Three months later, the Astoria, Ore.-based Morning Daily Herald ran a headline: "The Oregon Improvement Company Is in Good Condition Again."

"Mr. Simon has sprung a great surprise on the public, and again attracted attention as a financier," the paper reported.

When Simon took over the company, the paper noted, "it was tottering over the abyss of bankruptcy, with hungry creditors eager to tear its various branches to pieces.... Mr. Simon unified all the various departments of the system, causing the railways, steamers and mines to cooperate, so as to earn money and show to the financial world that it possessed of great value." In 1897, the Oregon Improvement Co. was reorganized as the Pacific Coast Company.

Simon was active in banking. He was a founder and director of Security Savings & Trust Co., a board member of Portland Trust Co. and First National Bank of Portland, a founder of the First National Bank of Southern Oregon and an investor in the Pacific Coast Joint Stock Land Bank of Portland, one of a chain of farm loan banks established to promote agriculture in the West.

He was among a group of investors who sought to bring Portland a first-class hotel: the Portland Hotel, which opened in 1890.

Simon also had extensive land holdings. By 1920, he was the largest Jewish land owner in Portland, William Toll wrote in "Making of an Ethnic Middle Class: Portland Jewry Over Four Generations."

Simon was a director of the Southwest Portland Real Estate Co., which offered "choice" residential lots with views of Mount Hood and Mount St. Helens. Houses could be bought in the late 1880s for $50 down and 14 monthly payments of $25 each.

While Simon was a successful lawyer with diverse and profitable business interests, it was his rapid rise in politics that brought him fame — and scorn.

CHAPTER TWO
Simon's meteoric rise

In 1877, Simon, at age 26, was elected to the Portland City Council, becoming its youngest member.

Three years later, he was chairman of the Oregon GOP, overseeing efforts statewide to elect Republicans.

``Simon's meteoric rise in the city, party and state politics was unprecedented,'' Tom Marsh wrote in ``To the Promised Land: A History of Government and Politics in Oregon.''

Simon benefited from his ties to his politically well-connected law partners and friends and his powerful railroad clients. He also rose fast because of his own ambition, determination and political skills.

He spent three years on the City Council where cutting "municipal extravagance" became one of his signature issues. Portland at the time had about 15,000 residents.

Simon's tenure on the council was marked by his sponsorship of an 1879 resolution seeking to crack down on city contractors employing Chinese on public works projects to ``the detriment of the white laboring class.''

Oregon's Legislature had passed a law prohibiting the employment of Chinese on public works projects. But ``cunning contractors'' sought to evade the law, the Evening Telegram reported.

The courts struck down the law. But virulent anti-Chinese sentiment continued, erupting into violence. Simon, as a U.S. senator, moved to crack down on Chinese immigration.

Just as Simon was on hand for the clanging of the bell from the transcontinental railroad's arrival, he was present for the ringing of the first telephones in Portland in 1878, two years after Alexander Graham Bell patented his invention. The City Council, during Simon's tenure, granted telephone companies the right to string wires on city streets.

Simon's council service came during a tumultuous time. One councilman was expelled for immoral conduct, and the police chief was censured for malfeasance in office and ``gross neglect of duty.''

On a lighter note, the threat posed by bean shooters was among the issues Councilman Simon faced.

``The boys in this city have become so skilled in their use that they can kill pigeons and even chickens with ease,'' the Oregonian warned. Bean shooters also were a menace to shopkeepers' windows.

The City Council passed a law providing for a jail sentence of up to 10 days and fine of up to $20 for using, or encouraging the use, of bean shooters.

Among Simon's official assignments was to respond to a letter from a New York woman asking about opportunities for women in Oregon.

``After considerable merriment, the communication was referred to Councilman Simon (he being the youngest member and single man),'' the Oregonian reported.

In perhaps the high point of Simon's days on the City Council, Portland welcomed former President Ulysses S. Grant to the city in 1879. Councilman Simon got to ride in the parade with the Civil War hero.

``Never before has Portland been so gaily decorated,'' the Oregonian reported. The streets were packed, with Portland's entire fire department—all five companies—turning out ``with their steam engines gaily trimmed and decked with flags and ribbons,'' the Daily Alta California reported.

Simon declined to seek reelection to the City Council, even though the Democratic party assured him that he would face no opposition.

``The Second Ward, in which he then lived, was almost united in its desire for him to serve again,'' the Oregonian reported.

Instead, he ran for the state Senate.

In the late 1870s and early 1880s, Simon served as a volunteer fireman and president of the Board of Delegates, overseeing an all-volunteer fire department. As a state senator, he introduced legislation creating the paid Portland Fire Department.

When Simon served as a volunteer fireman, "his most frustrating experience was the great conflagration in 1873 that consumed twenty city blocks—practically the entire downtown district," according to Rabbi Julius J. Nodel's "The Ties Between: A Century of Judaism on America's Last Frontier," a story of Portland's Congregation Beth Israel. "All that Joseph Simon and his crew could do was save lives and prevent further spreading of the flames."

The largest fire in Portland's history burned for 12 hours.

Simon's fondness for the fire service was apparent during his mayoralty.

He invited firemen to call at his office "at any hour of the day." After his administration ordered the first "motor-driven apparatus" for the fire department, he was there for the test, holding on as the engine reached 50 miles per hour.

Simon began his ascent in the Republican party in the mid-1870s, working to elect Rutherford B. Hayes as president.

He worked his way up the party hierarchy—county chairman, state committee member, secretary of the Republican State Central Committee and, finally, state party chairman. He later served as a national Republican committee member.

"In 1878 as secretary of the Republican State Central Committee, he managed the campaign so successfully that in 1880 he was made chairman of the committee. It was at that time that his marked ability as a leader and political general first received recognition," according to the Oregon Blue Book.

Simon was credited with helping engineer the Republican takeover of the Oregon Legislative Assembly. Republicans kept control of the Oregon House of Representatives until 1935 and the state Senate until 1957.

"The Republican party is Joe Simon, and Joe Simon is the Republican party," the Oregonian wrote in 1891.

"The real test of a man's Republicanism if he is to run for office," added the Corvallis Gazette, "is, 'Is he satisfactory to Joseph Simon?'"

Simon was a delegate at the 1892 Republican convention in Minneapolis, supporting William McKinley for the party's presidential nomination.

McKinley, ironically, would later use the campaign slogan, "The

People Against the Bosses." President Benjamin Harrison, however, won the nomination.

In 1880, Simon was elected to the state Senate from Multnomah County, which includes Portland.

At the time, Portland, with a population of about 17,500, was the largest city in the Northwest.

The city in 1880 welcomed Rutherford B. Hayes in the first presidential visit to the Pacific Coast.

Simon, a rising star in the GOP, likely met the president when Hayes visited the state Capitol.

Hayes went onto Portland where thousands turned out for his appearance. With Simon's law partner and mentor Joseph N. Dolph among the president's hosts, Simon also probably met General William Tecumseh Sherman, who accompanied Hayes on his 71-day western tour.

A year later, the 30-year-old Simon launched a bid for mayor of Portland.

The Oregonian, which spoke glowingly of Simon as a state Senate candidate, was less enthusiastic about his mayoral bid.

``Those who want a man who has shown his will to serve the people rather than party, and to advance the interests of the city rather than the interests of politicians and office-seekers, will not vote for Simon," the paper wrote.

Long before anyone ever heard of hanging chads, Portland's razor-thin mayor's race produced a Simon victory, then defeat, a recount, and then, naturally, a court fight.

When the ballots were first counted in the 1881 election, Simon was declared the winner – by nine votes.

He even took the oath of office.

But a counting error was found, and Mayor David Thompson was declared the winner — by a single vote.

A recount was ordered amid allegations of fraud.

``Both sides claim that the other corruptly influenced voters by the wholesale use of money and agree that never was a more disgraceful election held in Portland," the Eugene City Guard reported.

``Each party accuses the other of corruption," the State Rights

Democrat of Albany, Ore., said in reporting on the contested election, adding: "And no doubt they are all correct in their charges."

So careless were election workers that an unsealed ballot box sat in a restaurant while they dined.

Simon contested the vote tally to the City Council.

The drama heightened when Councilman William H. Andrus, who would help decide the outcome, was accused of betting on a Simon victory in the election.

Andrus admitted that he placed wagers on the race, but for friends, not for himself, and said that he had no personal financial stake in the outcome. (Betting on elections was a common practice. "Election Betting Lively," read a 1902 Oregonian headline.)

Newspapers alleged that councilmen had been offered payoffs to throw the election to Simon.

"The bribery employed in the election was frightful," the Oregonian wrote.

One councilman was reportedly offered $2,500 in cash and told that if Simon became mayor, he would receive an additional $10,000 in city contracts.

After the Oregonian ran a story on the reported bribes, Simon stopped by the newspaper's offices to declare he knew nothing of payoffs and welcomed an investigation.

"We have not asserted that any attempt has been made to bribe members of the Common Council with Mr. Simon's knowledge or sanction, nor do we think he would give his sanction to such an act," the paper wrote.

Emotions ran high, with Simon and Thompson exchanging sharp words at a council meeting.

The election came down to a single ballot.

Thompson's name was printed on the ballot, Simon's name was written in pencil, but no names were scratched out.

"Whether it shall be thrown out or whether counted for Joseph Simon will decide who shall be the head of government in Portland for the coming three years," the Oregonian wrote.

Simon contended the ballot should be counted for him.

But the council tossed out the ballot.

The council, after its recount, determined the race was tied, 1,783 to 1,783.

That handed victory to the incumbent, who was entitled to continue to hold office until a successor is ``duly elected.''

Simon challenged the council decision in court but lost. The court ruled that the council was, according to the city charter, the final arbiter of mayoral elections.

``It is said that Mr. Simon bears his defeat graciously, thinking, no doubt, of the 'whirligig of time that brings about its revenges,''' the Oregon Sentinel reported, quoting Shakespeare.

The prediction of future payback would prove spot on.

Several years later, Thompson ran for governor and lost, declaring that he had been ``knifed'' by Simon and his friends.

Simon was accused of backing Thompson's Democratic opponent.

``Simon always had it in for Thompson for defeating him for mayor, and has at last had his revenge,'' the Astorian wrote.

Simon also later played a key role in ousting Oregon Chief Justice John B. Waldo, who wrote the decision upholding the ruling against Simon in the mayoral contest.

After his painful loss in the mayor's race, Simon returned to the state Senate where he served until 1892. He retired to devote his full attention to his law practice. But two years later, he returned to the state Senate after friends and fellow Republicans urged him to run again. He continued serving until his election to the U.S. Senate in 1898.

Early in his political career, Simon had ``heavy chin whiskers,'' according to the 1882 book ``Pen Pictures of Representative Men of Oregon.'' Hubert Howe Bancroft, in "Chronicles of the Builders of the Commonwealth," described Simon as having a dark brown beard. Later, Simon wore a moustache.

Simon served five times as state Senate president.

To get a sense of his power, consider this: In 1897 and 1898, 24 of the 30 state senators were Republicans, and their leader was Joe Simon. The remaining six senators were divided equally between Democrats and Populists.

Legislative sessions generally lasted 40 days.

Oregon Senate, Joseph Simon, center. The Oregon Mist, 1895. Courtesy
of the University of Oregon's Oregon Newspaper Project.

In the late 1880s, money flowed ``like water into the pockets and
down the throats of legislators," as Tom Marsh put it in ``To The Promised
Land: A History of Government and Politics in Oregon."

``Two-and-a-half dollar gold pieces were the favorite considerations
for votes—they were small and easily palmed," Burton Hendrick wrote
in McClure's Magazine.

Newspapers outside of Simon's political base of Portland often accused
the state Senate president of putting the interests of his corporate clients
and political supporters ahead of the public's welfare.

The Roseburg Review in 1898 called Simon's election as Senate
president a victory for the ``wealthy, brainy and selfish men of Portland
who seek to control the destinies of that city and of the state in their own

personal interests and utterly and contemptuously regardless of the plain people."

"Joe Simon is boss of the Republican Party at Portland and that means that he is the boss of the party in the state," wrote the Albany Democrat.

But the Corvallis Gazette praised Simon.

"It is contemptible to accuse Joe Simon with being a fiend incarnate because he is a successful politician," the paper wrote. It called him "one of the best presiding officers the Oregon Senate has ever honored with the position."

The Oregonian also praised Simon.

"He has stood between Multnomah County and a determined effort on the part of the rest of the state to saddle upon this community an unjust and unequal share of the burden of the state's maintenance," the paper wrote.

In 1887, the Oregonian reported that the "most powerful force in the legislature is the Portland ring of which State Senator Simon is the manager.... The ring itself in the legislature is small, consisting of only a few men, but they are adroit men, experienced both in legislation and in political management, and always able to force a majority whenever the matter at issue is urgent."

Simon was described by the Inter Ocean newspaper as having "a hand of iron with a touch of velvet."

Among Simon-sponsored measures that passed the Legislature was a bill authorizing construction of a railroad bridge across the Willamette River between Portland and East Portland.

The measure, described by the Oregonian as "near and dear" to Simon, was vetoed by Gov. Pennoyer, Simon's former teacher. But Simon, who learned his political lessons well, succeeded in persuading the Legislature to override the veto.

Portland's first railway bridge over the Willamette was another significant step in the city's progress. The Oregonian called the bridge bill important to the entire state.

Ferries were the common way across the Willamette until the first bridge—the Morrison bridge—opened in 1887. It was such a momentous occasion that about 20,000 people showed up for the "novelty" of walking across the bridge, the Sacramento Record-Union reported.

Another bill championed by Simon provided for leasing of the Oregon Railway and Navigation Company system to Union Pacific, "a measure that the people of the entire state deem of incalculable benefit," Bancroft wrote in "Chronicles of the Builders of the Commonwealth."

The Morning Oregonian cheered the railroad lease as ushering in a "new era in the history of Oregon."

"New markets will be opened for millions of dollars' worth of Oregon products," the paper wrote.

Among the laws enacted during Simon's time in the statehouse were measures to allow women to practice law, prohibit the sale of tobacco to minors under age 18, and create a fund to keep Indian war veterans and Oregonians who served in the Union army during the Civil War "out of the poor house."

Lawmakers also approved a measure to encourage tree planting in schools on Arbor Day "to stimulate the minds of children" on the benefits of preserving forests and growing timber.

Also approved were a measure authorizing counties to pay bounties for the scalps of wild animals, including not more than $10 nor less $2 for a wolf or coyote, and an act requiring counties, upon the petition of 100 voters, to submit to public vote the question: "Shall swine be allowed to run at large?"

Looking back on his state Senate career, Simon told the Oregonian, "I think my best service in the state Senate was in introducing just as few bills as possible and in keeping others from introducing bills."

Still, he won approval of a new Portland city charter that "placed almost unlimited power in the hands of the mayor," as Portland Mayor Thompson put it.

Jewell Lansing wrote in "Portland: People, Politics and Power" that Simon was "the brains behind many changes in Portland's city charter."

Simon sought changes to the city charter "so that in case he should succeed in his desire to become mayor, he would have increased powers in his hands," the Oregonian wrote shortly before Portland's 1881 mayoral election. (In 1906, Oregon voters—perhaps in response to Simon's political scheming—used the initiative to take the power to enact or amend city charters away from the Legislature and put it in the hands of city voters.)

Among Simon's legislative achievements was the creation of a police commission for Portland.

``The theory upon which the commission was created was a good one," the Morning Oregonian wrote in 1885, describing it as an effort at reform. But the paper called it unfortunate that the first commissioners were active in politics.

Simon, ever the clever politician, managed to have himself appointed to the three-member commission by Gov. Zenas F. Moody in 1885. He served on the panel until 1892.

The panel had ``all the powers of the czar of Russia," the Capital Journal wrote.

Simon was said to have used the power of the police force to push his personal and political agenda.

The commission was ``at the center of much of the local political corruption and bribery," E. Kimbark MacColl wrote in ``The Shaping of a City: Business and Politics in Portland, Oregon, 1885 to 1915."

During his days in the state Capitol, Simon often came under attack for kowtowing to the railroad industry.

While Simon worked for and invested in railroads, he was deeply involved in pushing legislation that affected the industry. When he was first elected to the state Senate, he chaired the railroad committee. As Senate president, he appointed the railroad panel's members.

This was, however, decades before the tough conflict-of-interest laws of today.

Simon was blamed for using his influence to make the state railroad commission a toothless body.

Railroad commission members had become ``captive to the pernicious influence of the railroads as represented by Joseph Simon, and fell like lackeys on their knees whenever he cracked the whip," the Portland Welcome newspaper asserted.

The Eugene City Guard, complaining about ``insufferable transportation charges," asked: ``With corporation attorney Jos. Simon at the helm and in control of the state Senate, who could hope for relief from grievous railroad extortion?"

The commission, widely criticized as useless, was finally abolished— with Simon's help.

Simon also was seen as doing the bidding of the railroads when, as Portland mayor, he vetoed an ordinance to sell bonds for public docks.

Railroads, some of whom were Simon clients, owned waterfront property, enabling them to control much of the shipping, including freight rates.

``It is a plain proposition for the people of Portland to hold the keys to their own gates rather than to permit railroad or private monopoly to hold them," the Oregon Journal opined.

Voters in 1907 authorized $500,000 in bonds for public docks so that shipping companies ``would not be compelled to pay the exorbitant dockage charges that are demanded by the privately owned docks," the Journal wrote.

Labor accused Simon of showing contempt for the voters, who had approved the bonds by a 2-1 margin.

Even Simon's usual business allies supported municipal ownership as vital to the city's hopes of taking advantage of the growth in commerce from completion of the Panama Canal. The Chamber of Commerce president called Simon's position ``incomprehensible," telling the Oregon Journal, ``He was elected to perform the will of the people."

Simon, a self-proclaimed guardian of the public's purse strings, contended that a municipal takeover of the docks would cost at least ten times more than projected, significantly adding to the city's debt, and needed more study. The Oregonian praised the mayor's ``conservative prudence."

The mayor dismissed the bond vote, telling the Oregon Journal that people have used the initiative to pass ``a lot of fool laws."

The Oregon Journal framed the issue as larger than municipal ownership of docks.

``The people of Portland are on trial," the paper wrote. ``It is simply a question now of whether they are capable of governing themselves or whether they must have persons in the city hall to benevolently boss and govern them. It is not a question of docks, vital as docks are, but a graver question of rights."

Ultimately, city voters used the initiative to clear the way for municipal ownership of docks, authorizing an even higher bond issue

``so the city might be freed from corporation control of the waterfront,''
as the Oregon Journal put it.

Simon was credited with pushing through legislation in 1885 that
created the Portland Water Committee, whose mission was to provide
the growing city with ``an abundance of good, pure and wholesome
water.''

The water board was ``probably the most constructive political move
in Joe Simon's long career. It was to result in Portland developing one of
the purest water systems in the United States,'' MacColl wrote.

Before the city established a purer water supply, it relied on water
pumped from the Willamette River, into which waste from upstream
mills and towns was dumped.

``Anyone with half a head realized that as the Valley filled up with
people and the quantity of sewage emptied into the river increased, the
danger from typhoid fever epidemics would be great,'' the Oregonian
noted.

Simon fought Gov. Pennoyer over legislation to allow Portland to
sell tax-exempt bonds for a project to bring water to Portland from the
mountains. Farmers and other rural interests objected that they would
be subsidizing Portland's water system if the bonds were exempt from
state taxation. The bonds even became an issue in the 1890 gubernatorial
election.

The legislature passed the tax-free bond measure twice, and Pennoyer
vetoed each.

Finally, Pennoyer signed the bonding measure after the tax exemption
was dropped.

Simon, in a 1922 interview with the Oregonian, called the water
bonds ``one of the most important pieces of legislation ever passed in
Oregon.'' Portland would eventually bring water from the Bull Run
watershed in the Cascade Mountains. It still provides Portland with most
of its water.

``I took a large part in the fight,'' Simon said, ``and we won. Gov.
Pennoyer told me one day that Bull Run water would give consumers of
it the goiter. Time has long since proved he was wrong.''

Once the Bull Run water arrived in 1895, Pennoyer, in a display of political chutzpah, was on hand for the ceremony. He drank the water and shrugged at its taste.

When "pure water" began flowing from city taps, the Oregonian called it "one of the greatest boons" to Portland. Officials said they also saw a reduction in typhoid cases.

Senate sessions could be treacherous with shouting, desk pounding and threats of violence.

During a heated 1885 debate, the sergeant-at-arms stepped in to prevent an enraged Democratic senator W.R. Bilyeu from assaulting Simon. Some newspapers reported that Bilyeu was preparing to pull a pistol on Simon.

"When it is considered that Bilyeu is a six-footer, and Simon a small man, the act was cowardly," the Oregonian wrote.

Bilyeu denied that he was moving to attack Simon or was packing heat.

Simon drew press scrutiny when the Oregon Legislature in 1891 considered a key election reform – the so-called Australian ballot – providing for a secret ballot.

The thinking was that if voters cast ballots in the privacy of booths, it would put an end to vote buying.

"The man who would offer a bribe can never be sure the goods are delivered," wrote the Dalles Weekly Chronicle.

Newspapers accused Simon of pushing amendments in order to weaken the bill and preserve his political power.

"It would seem that the ballot reform law, which has proven so successful and altogether satisfactory in other states where tried, ought to be good enough for Oregon without any of Mr. Simon's amendments tacked on," the Newberg Graphic wrote.

In the end, the measure passed – with Simon's support.

In those days, lawmaking wasn't a full-time job, and Simon was still tending to his law practice.

In 1893, he represented a defendant in a sensational case in which more than two dozen people were accused of smuggling as many as 1,500 Chinese laborers and more than two tons of opium into the United States.

A number of the defendants were convicted, including Simon's client, C.J. Mulkey, a former Treasury agent sentenced to a year in jail.

Simon also advocated on behalf of a convicted killer's release from prison.

The case was ``one of the most celebrated in the criminal annals of Oregon," the Lebanon Express wrote.

In 1885, Wirt W. Saunders shot and killed Charles Campbell in Albany, Ore.

The two young men got into an argument after Saunders' fiancé's sister accused Campbell of harassing her. Saunders claimed self-defense. He was convicted of murder and sentenced to life in prison.

Simon was among influential Oregonians who signed a petition to Gov. Pennoyer urging Saunders' release.

After spending 10 years behind bars as a model prisoner, Saunders was freed on condition that he leave the state and never return.

Saunders went on to become a judge in Washington.

``From Scaffold to Bench," read a headline in the Inter Ocean newspaper.

Newspapers praised Saunders' transformation. But when it came to Joe Simon, the press wasn't as kind to the political boss as it was to the convicted killer.

CHAPTER THREE
``Worse than a Southern Pacific train robber''

During his long political career, Simon was called a ``political dictator,'' ``King Joe Simon,'' a ``clever underneath fighter,'' ``the self-crowned ruler of Portland,'' ``supreme boss of his party,'' and ``slippery little Joe Simon.''

He was assailed as ``a man who has done more to corrupt the Republican politics of this state than any other man living or dead,'' a ``man whose political record would disgrace a Tammany chief,'' and ``the most corrupt of politicians.''

He was attacked as a ``most unprincipled ward heeler,'' ``the wrecker of party harmony,'' ``enemy of reform,'' ``political pirate,'' a ``rotten politician,'' a ``very bad, scoundrelly man,'' and a ``man altogether unlovely politically in the eyes of the people.''

And there were the more endearing terms: ``schemer,'' ``weasel,'' ``leach,'' ``scurvy villain,'' ``political misfit,'' ``the little man who says nothing, but does a whole lot,'' and a ``shrewd little squirrel of a corporation lawyer.''

There was no dispute that he was ``the man through whom things are done,'' as the Oregonian put it.

Simon was an ``intense, ambitious, 'wheeler-dealer' of great personal charm,'' E. Kimbark MacColl wrote in ``The Shaping of a City: Business and Politics in Portland, Oregon, 1885-1915.''

The Boss was accused of using his position to enrich himself, putting the interests of railroad clients, friends and political supporters ahead of the public's welfare, engaging in dirty tricks and treachery, betraying his party and offering ``boodle'' to secure votes.

``He has controlled the Republican machinery in the interests of his employing corporations,'' the East Oregonian wrote.

``Joe is the most absolute boss his party has ever had in this state,'' wrote the State Rights Democrat.

``He manages to manipulate the party organization in the interest of himself and his favorite henchmen,'' the paper wrote.

Simon's hold on Portland was ``like the grip of a vice,'' the Oregon Journal wrote.

``It dictated nominations, controlled officials, made slates for state conventions, and in a general way substituted itself for the people in the exercise of power,'' the paper wrote.

Simon faced relentless attacks. Among them:

``Joseph Simon is the Judas Iscariot of Oregon politics. We apologize to Mr. Iscariot for the use of his name in this connection.''—The Astorian.

``If it is possible to induce Joe Simon to change his residence to some other state, the Blade would heartily be in favor of it, no matter what the cost would be. 'Little Joe' has undoubtedly caused more trouble, in a political way, than any other ten men in the state.''—-Baker City Blade.

``There isn't a more unscrupulous or more corrupt politician west of the Rocky Mountains.''—Oregon Courier.

``The Simon ring is a disgrace to the state of Oregon.... The ring dominates Multnomah County to such an extent that every man on the regular Republican ticket is a Simon tool.''—La Grande Chronicle.

``It is becoming evident every day that Joe Simon is the Republican Party of Oregon. To do his bidding, to be his lackey, is the sole requirement asked of a legislative candidate.'' – La Grande Chronicle again.

``Someday, we hope, we will get a legislature of the people, by the people and for the people, instead of by Joe Simon.''—Lincoln County Leader.

``No matter what happens Simon always comes out on top and when he says wiggle waggle, wiggle waggle goes.''—-The Dalles Chronicle.

``It is devoutly to be prayed that the people of Oregon will bid goodbye to Joseph Simon and relegate him to the obscurity he and his methods deserve. He has been a blight upon the name of Oregon. He has debauched voters. He has prostituted the noble right of suffrage…. He has spread disease germs throughout the body politic…. His name and career might be utilized by mothers to frighten babies."—the East Oregonian.

``For many years, Mr. Simon has represented the element that follows the principle that 'the end justifies the means.'"—the East Oregonian again.

``Simon cares nothing for the Republican Party and has never hesitated to knife the ticket to accomplish political ends."—Oregon City Enterprise.

``Just as it is pretty hard to teach an old dog new tricks, just so it is useless to expect Mr. Simon to inaugurate any reform in state affairs."— Hillsboro Argus.

``The people of Oregon have absolutely no use for Simon, who, apart from being nothing but a most unprincipled ward heeler, is of no more service to Oregon than a fifth wheel is to a coach."—The Dalles Daily Chronicle.

``Simony, in English law, is sale of a benefit. Simony, in Oregon politics, is sale of a party." – The Oregonian.

``Joe Simon has been mentioned as a compromise senator. Save the people."—The State Rights Democrat.

``He gains his elections by methods which will not bear scrutiny and his name, as a politician, is a by-word in the mouths of street gamins – and yet, with a tenacity unequalled in the history of the state, he holds his grip on the state's affairs."—The Hillsboro Argus.

``Mr. Simon has never had a reform idea in his brain. His hair does not curl that way. He is simply a smooth boss and corporation lawyer. He uses the Republican party to feather his own nest."—the Daily Capital Journal.

``He has probably done more in Portland to disrupt the Republican party than any man there."—Albany Democrat.

``Simon (we mean Joe) says wig wag, and the whole machinery of the Republican Party in Multnomah County is set in motion in obedience to the mandate of the Republican 'Boss.'…He manages to carry the Republican Party in his pocket for his own benefit."—Albany Democrat again.

``Mr. Simon has been able to give a most surprising demonstration of the great truth that, to succeed as a candidate, it is not necessary to run fast, or to be much of a vote-getter. The main point is to make sure that the other fellow—the opposing candidate—is hobbled in some way, and gets fewer votes."—the Morning Oregonian.

"If this man had one conception of decency, he would make no futile attempt to further thrust himself upon the people. Figuratively speaking, they should grab him by the back of the neck and the slack of his pants and pitch him from his political pedestal for all time to come. He has prostituted the politics of Oregon long enough."—East Oregonian.

"In nothing that Mr. Simon has accomplished politically can we find that he has served the people of Oregon, or the state itself, but in everything we hear the voice of Jacob and feel the hand of Esau. He has become a political misfit, and he must step aside and leave the public work to be done by more unselfish and patriotic hands."—East Oregonian.

"Simonism, as this city, county and state know to their sorrow, is something from which to flee as from contagion."—Oregon Journal.

"Simonism and corruption are synonymous terms."—Corvallis Gazette.

"Joe Simon is a bad man."—the Capital Journal.

Newspapers were often brutal.

"The people don't want Joe Simon for an absolute King and Dictator of this great commonwealth," the East Oregonian wrote. "There isn't a drop of responsive, fairly representative human blood in that little machine boss' carcass."

"In what single, solitary moral or material manner has Simon helped Oregon?" the East Oregonian wrote another time. "His sole energy has been to selfish ends; if he wore a mask of public spirited righteousness for a moment, it was to accomplish a blacker deceit and more wholesale betrayal. The evil effects of his practices will remain for years, like an uncovered sewer, in Oregon political affairs."

One of the more amusing attacks on Simon appeared in a correction published in the Evening Capital Journal: "The Journal editorial referring to Hon. Joseph Simon as the 'richly rewarded tool of the corruptionists' does that gentleman grave injustice. By error of typesetting and in proof reading, the word which was written 'corporationists' was changed. We had not any intention to charge Mr. Simon with corruption."

And then there was this nugget from the Oregonian:

``If there is any man who thinks that Mr. Simon is an able and efficient man in the United States Senate, has served the state as well as anybody could, that the Senate is a proper place for him, that he is a proper man for the place, and that Oregon couldn't do better....let him enjoy his opinion. But he will be fortunate in one thing. He will not be troubled by the press of the crowd around him."

Simon's reputation extended beyond Oregon.

``There is no state in the Union wherein the one-man power is so potent, where the ballot box is so boldly tampered with, or where votes are so openly marketed as in Oregon," the Denver Times wrote in 1898.

Boss Simon was likened to New York's corrupt Tammany Hall bosses. ``Oregon is the blackest black sheep in our flock, thanks to the gold of Portland's biggest bank and the machinations of Boss Simon," the Denver Times wrote.

Simon supporters were called Simonites, Simon Republicans and the Simon gang. The Oregonian called them the ``Simon Mafia."

Simon was widely regarded as an astute politician, even by critics.

"As a political organizer, it is doubtful if he has an equal on the Pacific coast," the Seattle Post-Intelligencer wrote.

The Inter Ocean newspaper in Chicago called him the ``keenest politician in Oregon." The Statesman Journal called him ``one of the brainiest men in the state" and a ``superb tactician."

``Mr. Simon has as many vigorous haters as any man in Oregon, but he also has myriads of cordial friends," the Oregon Statesman wrote, ``and it can be said that there is scarcely a man in the state who enjoys the confidence of prominent businessmen and capitalists to such an extent as he does."

While Simon was ``clearly the most powerful individual in Oregon politics from 1880 to 1910, he was ``not 'the Boss,' as his detractors claimed," E. Kimbark MacColl wrote in ``Merchants, Money and Power: The Portland Establishment, 1843-1913."

``He had to barter and bargain to achieve his goals," MacColl noted. ``Simon continually struggled to exercise control over the state and local political machinery of a party that was splintered into various factions until 1905."

"There is little evidence that he used influence or political patronage in a manner different from other practical politicians," Tony H. Evans wrote in his UC Berkeley dissertation "Oregon Progressive Reform, 1902-1914."

Just how Machiavellian Simon was can be difficult to determine, given how partisan the newspapers were at the time.

Simon ward heelers were accused of rounding up people to cast ballots for their slates, whether they were eligible to vote or not.

"One glint of gold in the hands of a hobo will prove that illegal voting is not without its reward," the Oregonian reported.

On the eve of an election, the Dalles Chronicle reported on the presence of a "large number of strange men" in Portland, "who, it is charged, have been brought here for the sole purpose of voting both early and often."

"Names have been put on the registration books which have no place there, and which were put there by the Simon machine," the Oregonian asserted. The paper said that many of the voters registered by the Simon machine "cannot be found at the place from which they are registered."

There was no effective registration law until 1899. "This allowed ballot box stuffing on a massive scale, with packs of professional voters wandering from poll to poll.... The outright purchase of votes was also a flourishing business," the Statesman Journal wrote.

"And if the purchase of votes from individual citizens was quite common, it was no less so from elected legislators," the paper wrote. "Oregon was no worse than other states, for this was the spirit of the times."

The Oregonian accused the Simon machine of paying for "repeaters," voters who cast ballots in more than one place.

Under the Simon machine, "rightful voters were often barred from the polls and imported rabble of the worst type brought into Portland and illegally used at the ballot box," the Oregon Journal wrote.

Vote buying was a common accusation at the time.

Or, as the Oregon Mist put it, men were bought like sheep.

"Voters were regularly bought for $2.50 a piece," Tom Marsh wrote in "To The Promised Land: A History of Government and Politics in Oregon."

The Daily Evening Bulletin in San Francisco reported in 1881 on a man arrested for bribery "in handing a voter $2.50 in consideration of his voting for Joseph Simon for mayor."

"Several other prominent persons were seen to purchase votes, and their names will be furnished to the district attorney for prosecution," the paper reported. There was no suggestion, at least in that instance, that Simon was engaged in the vote-buying.

The Oregonian in 1886 reported on the arrest of several men for allegedly buying votes and noted: "The bribers were promptly bailed by Hon. Joseph Simon."

In an 1890 Portland election, the "price for votes" began at $2.50, but in the final hours of balloting, with both sides confident of the outcome, "only $1 was paid in some places," the Oregonian reported.

The Oregon Journal, in a story on prisoners escaping from the courthouse through a hole in the floor of the grand jury room, recalled how the hole was previously used during a heated election between Simon and Mitchell forces to sneak prisoners into the courthouse to vote.

"The precinct was carried for the Simon ticket," John F. Logan, the law librarian, told the paper in 1904. "While the opposition was sore, it couldn't help laughing over the shrewdness of the trick."

In one election, the polls were packed with "hobos and floaters" by the Simon machine, making the lines so long as to discourage "actual citizens" from Portland from voting, according to the Capital Journal.

There also were reports of intimidation.

Even casting a ballot could be treacherous. At one crowded polling place in Portland, a man had an ear cut off by a razor, the Oregon Statesman reported.

Simon's bare-knuckles political style was enough of a concern that the Oregonian warned in bold letters prior to a 1902 election, "Look out for the ballot box stuffer tomorrow. Don't let Simon elect his delegates before the polls open or after they are closed."

The ballot stuffing and other misconduct wasn't limited to the Simon machine.

While the Simon machine was accused of pressuring voters through tactics such as dispatching pro-Simon police to polls on Election Day, Simon's enemies employed their own hardball methods. Portland's assistant postmaster W.F. Matthews, a Mitchell ally, was suspected of opening mail sent to Simon looking for anything that could be used against him.

"Sometimes it was Simon and sometimes Mitchell—but, whoever won, the methods were always the same—-bribery, fraud and violence," the St. Helen's Oregon Mist wrote.

``Which is the biggest dictator, Mitchell or Joe Simon, it is difficult to decide," wrote the Albany Democrat.

The Oregon Journal in 1904 reported on fraudulent voter registrations on a ``very large scale" by both Simon and Mitchell supporters.

Sometimes, however, Simon drew praise from newspapers.

``One of the chief causes of Simon's success as a politician was his fidelity to his promises," the Capital Journal wrote. ``A political promise made by Mr. Simon was never broken."

The Oregonian wrote in 1884 that Simon's ability and fitness for the legislature are ``conceded even by his opponents."

``Multnomah has never sent to the legislature a man of brighter or more active mind, or one better fitted for practical work. And besides, there is the utmost confidence in his integrity," the paper said.

``Whether in his office, trying a case, or as a legislator at Salem or Washington, he is never on parade but always at work," the Capital Journal wrote in 1899. ``He never struts before the pubic. He just works."

The Oregonian defended Simon from the attacks of bossism.

``Every little office-seeking and grafting politician, who has been disappointed in reaching the objective he has sought, feels that he must have someone to blame for his disappointment. So he howls `Simon,'" the paper wrote in endorsing Simon for reelection to the state Senate in 1898.

``No dollar from the city or county treasury has ever gone into his pocket through office-holding, fees or emoluments," the paper added.

The Lincoln County Leader added: ``The fact that a man is successful makes him enemies, and it is largely that Joe Simon has been successful that he has so many enemies in his own party."

``The man that has no enemies will never be felt in the world of politics if in any other," the Oregon City Enterprise wrote.

``One admirable trait in Senator Simon's character," the Corvallis Gazette wrote, ``is that during all the years past in which the press of this state vilified him, he did not fight back but silently endured the scourge, without complaint, without excuse or attempt to palidate or justify himself for the heinous charges made against him."

The Corvallis Gazette also wrote that Simon, through his political life, was "remarkably free from any just charge of supreme selfishness" and called him a "man of irreproachable character."

Simon was a "master of details" and "the hardest worked official in Oregon," Colonel E. Hofer, editor of the Capital Journal, wrote after Simon was elected mayor of Portland.

"He gets all over the city," the paper added. "Nothing escapes his attention, and for the first time in their lives, the organized array of municipal grafters are up against the real thing." The editorial praised Simon for leaving a law practice "worth at least $50,000 a year" to bring order out of chaos at City Hall.

"Tenacity of purpose is one of his characteristics," the Oregonian wrote.

Simon rarely granted interviews.

"Mr. Simon is not a talkative man," the Oregon Daily Journal wrote.

"I do not care to be interviewed," he told a reporter for the newspaper in 1902. "My work will speak for itself and action counts more than words."

Newspapers were filled with stories accusing him of engaging in political mischief, and rarely was there a response from him.

"Pioneer editors did not mince words," the Oregon Statesman Journal reported in a 1959 centennial edition looking back on the state's early days. "Most were all-out Democrats or Republicans...Villains from the opposing party were castigated viciously."

"It seems that when anything goes wrong nowadays that everybody blames me for it," Simon told the Oregonian in 1890.

Perhaps that explains Simon's view, as reported by the Astorian, that he would "feel better if there were no reporters or newspapers."

Simon benefitted, and then suffered, at the hands of the influential Oregonian, which shared his support for the gold standard. The Republican newspaper often supported Simon during his days in the state Capitol and mayor's office but strongly opposed his bid for reelection to the U.S. Senate.

The rival Oregon Journal called out the Oregonian for "inconsistent" treatment of Simon and blamed Oregonian editor Harvey Scott's U.S. Senate ambitions for besmirching the "good record" of Senator Simon. It was a surprising defense of Simon given that the Journal became a sharp thorn in Simon's side.

Among the provocative headlines attacking Simon were "Mayor Guilty, But Not Sorry About It" (from the Oregon Journal) and "Portland's Executive Sought Extraordinary Means to Influence Confirmation" (East Oregonian).

Both headlines referred to a Simon effort to persuade the U.S. Senate to appoint a fellow thirty-third degree Mason to a federal position. Simon sent a telegram to a former Senate colleague and fellow Mason asking if there were "not enough of us thirty-thirds" in the Senate to secure the federal appointment.

The Journal took Simon to task for his telegram.

"When he employed Free Masonry for political purposes, Mayor Simon made an inexcusable blunder," the paper wrote.

The East Oregonian wrote that the incident showed that Simon is "still the crafty politician he was in the days of machine rule."

Oregon Senator Jonathan Bourne expressed outrage at Simon's telegram.

He called it a "sad day" when Senate business is influenced "by the question of whether a man does or does not hold membership in a secret society," the East Oregonian reported. "In official appointments, the first test should be that of honesty; second, efficiency; third, political principles. There is no place for a test that involves religion, personal relationship or fraternal affiliation."

In 1891, Simon was under consideration for a $6,000-a-year lifetime seat on the U.S. Court of Appeals for the Ninth Circuit, which then took in the states of California, Idaho, Montana, Nevada, Oregon and Washington.

Some newspapers didn't like the idea at all.

"Joe Simon is a pretty big man for a little fella," the Spokane Review wrote. "He can boss the Republican delegation in Congress and the Democratic governor. It remains to be seen whether he can boss the president of the United States."

Simon had the support of an impressive list of officials, including Gov. Pennoyer, the state's congressional delegation, the state attorney general and several former judges. Pennoyer, in a letter to the president, called Simon "above reproach in his moral character, true to his friends and meriting the esteem of his fellow citizens."

The Oregonian supported another candidate for the judgeship, but still praised Simon for possessing "an active mind, an imperturbable temper, good working habits, great aptitude for business and good knowledge of law."

But the Astorian, among the newspapers which spoke out against Simon's appointment, wrote: 'So far as Oregon is concerned it is Joe Simon or nobody for circuit judgeship. Then let it be nobody."

The paper called Simon grossly unfit for the judgeship.

"It would be a discredit to Oregon and a disgrace to the bench to appoint such a dishonest political boss as Joe Simon is known to be," wrote the Daily Herald of Albany, Ore.

The Salem Journal warned Simon's appointment to the federal bench would cost Republican President Harrison Oregon in the next presidential election.

"If Oregon is to be made Democratic next year, there is no surer way to accomplish that end than to place Joe Simon on the federal bench," the newspaper warned. "The fact that a man can play the role of 'political boss' and manipulate bills in the legislature is certainly not a good recommendation for the position of United States circuit judge."

The Dalles Daily Chronicle added: "Simon is smart beyond question but his smartness lies in the direction of trickery and unscrupulous political bossism and that is poor material to make a judge out of."

The best argument for Simon's appointment to the bench, some newspapers wrote, was that it would remove him from Oregon politics.

"There is a possible ray of comfort growing out the probability of Joe Simon being appointed to a position on the federal bench. He says if he is appointed he will reside in San Francisco. This may prove bad for California but Oregon will be the gainer by it," wrote the Wasco County Sun.

"No, no, the country does not want federal judges whose chief qualification is that they are smart and unscrupulous political bosses," the Dalles Chronicle wrote, "but Oregon would be perfectly reconciled if Simon should go to California or—Canada."

Still, some newspapers supported Simon for the judgeship.

"We have had some hard things to say about Joseph, but we believe he has the stuff in him to make a good judge," opined the East Oregonian.

"He has a profusion of common sense, and that is one of the most important virtues of a competent and able jurist."

In response to criticism that Simon was a corporate lawyer, the Portland Evening Telegram wrote: "Any Republican who will be appointed to the federal judgeship will be a corporation attorney.... As long as that is settled, it might as well be Mr. Simon as anyone else, especially as long as he has more brains than any of the rest of them."

The U.S. Justice Department reportedly opposed Simon's appointment, further dimming his prospects.

In the end, the president appointed William B. Gilbert, another Portland attorney, as the first Oregonian to serve on the court.

"Every decent Republican in Oregon blushed for shame when the telegrams repeatedly announced that our senators were supporting Joe Simon" for the judgeship, the Dalles Chronicle wrote. "It is to the credit of President Harrison that the Simon medicine was too strong for his digestive organs."

Pennoyer's recommendation "did Simon no good," the Oregonian noted.

"The president has a good memory, and when he saw Pennoyer's name, he recalled the asinine performance of the Oregon governor as he was about to enter the borders of the state," the paper wrote.

It was a reference to the iconoclastic Pennoyer's refusal to travel to the Oregon border to welcome the president on his arrival in the state in 1891.

"If Harrison wants to see me, let him call on me at the state house, like any other visitor," Pennoyer remarked, according to "The Scrap Book.'" (Simon was among the officials who greeted President Harrison in a downpour on his arrival in Oregon. Simon also joined the president on stage when Harrison delivered a speech in Portland.)

Losing the appointment was a big disappointment to Simon, according to the Oregon Statesman, which called the judgeship "the dearest plum he ever coveted."

The Dalles Chronicle, a frequent Simon critic, praised Harrison's decision.

"Mr. Simon is a staunch Republican and an able lawyer but President Harrison, it would seem, does not consider these sufficient," the paper wrote. "If Mr. Simon's political methods, successful though they may have always been, were less shady, less liable to just criticism and more consistent and honorable, there cannot be a doubt he would have captured the judicial prize."

Some newspapers suggested Simon sought a measure of payback at Harrison by leading the Oregon delegation in supporting McKinley over Harrison at the 1892 Republican convention.

Simon, as political lighting rod, was also apparent during a tumultuous party convention he chaired in 1896.

"Convention Ends in Fierce Riot," read the Chicago Tribune headline.

Simon, as chairman of the Republican county central committee, was attempting to convene a party convention when an opposing Republican faction knocked him off the platform and attempted to seat its own man, Judge Charles H. Carey, as presiding officer.

"In a moment the hall was in an uproar," the Evening Telegram reported. "Where there has been comparative quiet, bedlam reigned. Mr. Joseph Simon, seizing a beer mallet, attempted to pound order from the pine table in front of him. His efforts were fruitless."

A fight broke out. "Canes were waved in the air and brought down on the heads of cursing, struggling men," the paper reported. "Blows were exchanged wherever elbow room could be gained to deliver them.

"'For five minutes, the battling, perspiring crowd surged up and down and across the stage," the newspaper continued.

The Oregonian reported that two of Carey's associates grabbed Simon by the throat and shoulders, pushing him to the back of the stage.

"The crowd piled on top of Simon and threatened to kill him," the Eugene City Guard reported.

"'Delegates rushed to their feet to the rescue of Mr. Simon, and a hand-to-hand struggle took place," the Dalles Chronicle reported.

Finally, tempers calmed, and a recess was declared.

Simon survived the turmoil. But a tougher fight lay ahead.

CHAPTER FOUR
``Truth Stranger Than Fiction"

Perhaps the most remarkable moment in Simon's political career was the way in which he engineered his rival John Mitchell's defeat and his own election to the U.S. Senate.

At the time, state legislatures chose U.S. senators.

Deadlocks were common. In one case, it took Oregon legislators 60 ballots to choose a senator with the vote coming only minutes before the Legislature was to adjourn.

Mitchell was expected to win reelection in 1897.

But Simon got an opportunity to take down his old foe, thanks to an unlikely alliance between two state representatives, Jonathan Bourne and William S. U'Ren.

Bourne, a Republican, and U'Ren, a Populist, were both lawyers, but they had very different backgrounds, personalities and political goals.

What they had in common was that they felt betrayed by Mitchell.

Bourne was upset with Mitchell for abandoning his support for free silver.

Mitchell changed his position after Republicans at their national convention included support for the gold standard in the party platform.

U'Ren was angry with Mitchell for reneging on a commitment to back the reformer's pet cause: establishing the initiative and referendum process.

(Publicly, Simon said he opposed Mitchell's reelection because he didn't trust his position on the money question, ``not regarding him as a safe and proper exponent of the principles of the Republican party.")

U'Ren and Bourne arranged for enough lawmakers—-a coalition of

Democrats, Populists, Silverites and so-called Simon Republicans—to stay away from the statehouse and prevent the House from mustering the necessary quorum to conduct business. Some lawmakers refused to take the oath of office.

They succeeded in bringing the legislature to a standstill in what became known as the great legislative Holdup of '97.

"In Oregon, the wheels of government ceased to turn," Hendrick wrote.

A letter writer to the Hood River Glacier complained that lawmakers "hid out longer than Noah's beasts were hidden in the ark."

"For forty days—the length of the session in Oregon—the lawmakers hung around the bar-rooms, or sat listlessly on the Capitol steps, spitting tobacco juice and swapping stories," Hendrick wrote.

Bourne offered rooms at a hotel to the fugitive lawmakers. "The hungry could find food, the thirsty, drink, and the lonely, companionship," former Governor Oswald West wrote years later in the Capital Journal.

In addition to the reports of debauchery, there were allegations of bribes to further encourage lawmakers to stay away from the statehouse.

Sergeants-at-arms were dispatched to bring fugitive lawmakers to the Capitol by force, if necessary. But the effort failed miserably.

The fugitives shrugged at the arrest warrants. A group of lawmakers signed onto a resolution declaring that it was impossible to compel the attendance of absent lawmakers "without great danger of bloodshed."

"If the members don't go, what am I to do?" Sergeant-at-Arms Glen Holman lamented, the Portland Telegram reported.

The Hillsboro Independent suggested that if the sergeant at arms could not compel absent lawmakers to report to the state Capitol, perhaps the National Guard should be called up.

The Portland Journal called the hold-up session "40 days of rotten putridity that will never be forgotten."

Tensions over the hold-up were so high that one lawmaker introduced a resolution seeking an evaluation of "the mental condition of Joe Simon." The resolution was ruled out of order.

Newspapers accused Bourne of maintaining a harem.

Lawmakers were kept drunk for weeks, and they congregated in places "where a decent and respectable woman could not go," George

Brownell, a former state senator, said in a 1910 speech looking back on the hold-up session.

"Never before in the history of any state in this Union has there been such a spectacle—such an assault on representative government," opined the Oregon Journal.

Hendrick called the hold-up "probably the most disgraceful episode in the whole history of American legislatures."

"Simonism, Bournism and populism have conspired against Republicanism," complained the Corvallis Gazette. "It is a case of boodle, lawlessness and anarchy arrayed against the representatives of decency, law and order and honest government."

"Disorganized Legislature," read a headline in the Capital Journal.

Some newspapers placed blamed for the hold-up session on Simon.

"President Simon, Dictator," screamed a headline in the Statesman Journal.

The Dalles Daily Chronicle wrote that Oregonians would "'long remember Joseph Simon, as the man, who more than anyone else, is most to blame for the deplorable" hold-up session

The Pendleton East Oregonian, however, assailed both Simon and Mitchell for the hold up.

"Simon is standing out on just as selfish grounds as Mitchell," the paper wrote. "His aims are no higher or nobler.... They are both politicians, struggling for power....They are both corruptionists and neither deserving of being entrusted with the affairs of state."

Simon and his allies were assailed for their "high-handed," "revolutionary," "obstructionist," and "cowardly" tactics. The "hold-up gang" also was attacked for "betraying those whom they were elected to serve."

"The delay in organization cannot be explained or excused on any grounds of law, honesty, public necessity or public good," the Corvallis Gazette wrote.

The Albany Herald wrote that the lawmakers refusing to take their seats, whether Republicans, Democrats or Populists, were "violating their duties and trampling upon the rights of the people of Oregon." The paper accused the lawmakers of acting like pirates.

The Oregon Statesman called the hold-up session "one of the most cunningly devised schemes ever hatched out in the caverns and recesses of hell."

The holder ups disputed the reports of Bacchanalian revelry.

U'Ren insisted that Bourne's entertaining was "the same that a gentleman offers to his guests in his own home in the presence of his wife and daughters."

A church leader who served in the state legislature and an Oregonian editor who covered the hold-up session also disputed the stories of wild partying.

Visitors to Bourne's hotel rooms were "royally entertained," the Oregonian reported. But the paper disputed that anything untoward occurred and attributed reports to the contrary as the work of Bourne's political enemies.

Bourne hired two cooks and a waiter, "fitted up a kitchen and dining room and entertained his friends as he would as if they were guests in his own home," the Hood River Glacier wrote. "His steward supplied the table with the best the markets afforded."

Mitchell assailed the "miserable anarchist scheme" that prevented the passage of any legislation for an entire session and deprived Oregon full representation in the U.S. Senate for a year and a half.

"The alliance between Bourne and U'Ren would become important to the future of politics in Oregon, but the short-term beneficiary was 'Little Joe' Simon," J.D. Chandler wrote in "Hidden History of Portland, Oregon."

The fact that U'Ren aided Simon's cause was stunning.

Only a few years earlier, the political reformer blamed the political boss for the legislature's defeat of U'Ren's proposal for an initiative and referendum.

"A wink from Joe Simon" was how U'Ren blamed the defeat, famed muckraker Lincoln Steffens wrote in his 1909 book "Upbuilders."

"U'Ren clearly understood one important point: that politicians are invariably opportunists, and look upon important public movements only as they affect their immediate personal interest," Hendrick wrote.

Spurring the drive for an initiative was public frustration with bosses like Simon and the power of the railroads, banks and other special interests.

"The people felt the government was getting away from them," Joseph N. Teal of Portland's Taxpayers League said at a 1909 conference on political reform.

"Legislatures and councils were too often more solicitous for special than for public interests and the people wanted to secure some effective and direct method of making their influence felt and their wishes respected."

(Oregon voters in 1902 overwhelmingly voted to establish the initiative and referendum process — with Simon's support. It's unclear whether Simon's endorsement was payment to U'Ren for helping engineer his election to the U.S. Senate or acknowledgement of the groundswell of support for political reform. Perhaps it was both.)

(The initiative and referendum were among reforms that came to be known as the "Oregon system" of direct democracy.)

(The initiative—a process that allows petitioners to bypass legislatures to put issues on the ballot—is now in effect in about half of the states. It has led to votes on just about every imaginable issue, from limiting taxes—California's Proposition 13 is the most famous—to Oregon's Death With Dignity Act. The referendum gives voters the opportunity to overturn legislation.)

With the Legislature deadlocked on the election of a U.S. senator, Gov. William P. Lord, a Republican, appointed 70-year-old Portland banker Henry W. Corbett to the Senate seat. Corbett, backed by Simon, was an Oregon pioneer who previously served in the U.S. Senate but lost his seat due to political maneuvering by Mitchell.

But the U.S. Senate, on a 50 to 19 vote, refused to seat Corbett.

The reason given by senators was that Corbett's seating would mean that "a minority could hold up a Legislature and throw the appointment of a United States senator into the hands of the governor," the New York Times reported. It also didn't help Corbett that many senators had served with Mitchell and regarded him as a friend.

The governor called a special session of the legislature. By then, Mitchell was no longer a candidate. Corbett withdrew his candidacy in an effort to ease the political tensions and end the stalemate.

That opened the door for Simon to make his move.

His fellow Republicans nominated him for U.S. senator. The next day, he was elected by the legislature.

"I have the pleasure, my fellow senators and representatives, of naming to you the next United States senator from the state of Oregon, the man who will cross the hills and plains and do valiant service for Oregon, for sound money and true Republicanism in the United States Senate in Oregon, the Honorable Joseph Simon," Sen. George Brownell said in nominating "the Little Giant of Oregon."

"Immense crowds thronged the statehouse" to witness the election, the Dalles Weekly Chronicle wrote.

The state Capitol was packed "almost to the degree of suffocation," the Oregonian reported.

Simon received the vote of every Republican who was present. He cast a blank ballot.

Cheering broke out in the chamber when the result was announced.

"There was a mad rush for the telegraph and telephone offices," the Oregonian reported.

"A Senator At Last," the Arizona Republic declared.

Simon told fellow lawmakers that he felt Corbett should have been elected, but he was, nevertheless, "deeply grateful" for the honor.

"Senator Simon took his honors very coolly and yet thoroughly enjoyed and appreciated the hearty congratulations he got on all sides," the Capital Journal reported. The paper called it a "great triumph" for Simon after he had been so "persistently fought, maligned and abused."

It must have delighted Simon to read the Astorian proclaim his election as a "complete and unqualified triumph" over the Mitchell forces.

On the train back to Portland, Simon was greeted by a large crowd at the Oregon City depot.

When he reached home, he was met by a brass band.

Shortly after his election, Simon wrote letters to editors addressed to Corbett.

"I really feel that I am occupying a position that rightfully belongs to you," Simon wrote. "The magnanimity displayed by you in retiring from the contest and permitting the election of a senator, instead of deadlocking the legislature, as you had the power to do, has endeared you to the Republicans of this state."

Still, some accused Simon of throwing Corbett under the bus.

The hold-up session—along with the belief that wealthy individuals bought Senate seats and cared more about their corporate benefactors than their constituents — galvanized public support for the election of U.S. senators by a direct vote of the people.

``If Oregon had direct lawmaking power through the ballot box there would be such reforms as would utterly rout Simonism," the Hillsboro Argus wrote.

Incidents in other states also gave momentum to the direct election of senators. When the Missouri Legislature in 1905 was debating who it would send to the U.S. Senate, a riot broke out ``in which bottles, books and spittoons were thrown," the St. Louis Republic reported.

Delaware went without any representation in the Senate from 1901 to 1903 when its legislature couldn't agree on who should represent the state.

Reformers contended that Simon never would have won the Senate seat by popular vote.

``A senator has been elected who could not have succeeded in an election before the people, one who is by no means the choice of a majority the voters of Oregon," the Dalles Times-Mountaineer said of Simon.

``The time is certainly approaching when the old, bunglesome method of electing senators will be abolished," the paper added.

George H. Haynes spotlighted Oregon's 1897 hold-up session in his 1906 book ``The Election of Senators."

``Not a bill of any kind could be passed, not even an appropriation for current expenses, so that while the regular taxes were bringing in a revenue, for fifteen months or more the bills of the state had to be paid in warrants drawing interest at eight percent," he wrote. ``Such is in the inglorious record of this American `Addled Parliament.'''

Some suggested that the popular election of senators might also improve the character of office holders. In the U.S. Senate during the 58th congressional session, ``at least one out of every ten members had been put on trial before the courts or subjected to legislative investigation for serious crimes or for grave derelictions from official duty," Haynes wrote.

The Oregon Legislative Assembly went on record as early as 1887 in support of the direct election of U.S. senators, declaring that selection of senators by legislatures was the ``cause of much contention and strife and even corruption."

Oregon lawmakers in 1901 took a step toward giving voters more say over the selection of U.S. senators. They passed a law allowing voters to express their preference for U.S. senators, but leaving the final decision to the legislature.

The law was pushed by Simon enemies in the belief it would end his Senate career "on the theory that he would not show up well in a popular vote," the Daily Journal reported.

The law was non-binding, however. In fact, the legislature chose a U.S. senator who didn't receive a single vote in the 1902 election.

Oregon voters then used the new initiative process in 1904 to pass a measure asking state legislative candidates to pledge to support the people's choice (actually the men's choice since women would not be granted the right to vote in Oregon until 1912) for U.S. senator, irrespective of party, or declare they would consider the public vote "as nothing more than a recommendation."

Soon after, the reform was put to the test. Remarkably, the Republican-controlled Legislature appointed a Democrat, Gov. George Chamberlain, the winner of the popular vote, to the Senate seat.

(Congress in 1912 approved the Seventeenth Amendment providing for the election of U.S. senators by a vote of the people and sent it to the states for ratification. It was added to the U.S. Constitution in 1913.)

Oregon's 1904 initiative also established the direct primary, allowing voters to nominate candidates.

It was aimed at party bosses like Simon and other members of "the inner ring that met in the back room and ruled the nominations," as the Oregonian put it. Through primary elections, voters will "take away from political bosses the power to control the distribution of offices," the Oregonian wrote.

The Mitchell faction "fathered the direct primary law so as to destroy Simon's political power," the Medford Tribune wrote in 1909. "It did, but once started, the movement for popular government couldn't be stopped," smashing both political machines.

Supporters of the direct primary quoted New York's notorious Boss Tweed to make their case: "You may elect whichever candidate you please to office, if you will allow me to select the candidates." Candidates nominated by voters, they argued in a 1904 pamphlet, "will more faithfully serve the people because their political life will depend always upon the people and no one else."

Not everybody was a fan of the direct primary. The Argonaut, a San Francisco-based journal, suggested the new nominating system would dissuade ``experienced, responsible men of exceptional talent'' from seeking public office and instead lead ``cranks, men inspired by vanities, nobodies swollen in their own deceit, necessitous creatures who want the emoluments of office'' to endeavor to put their names on the ballot.

Among the skeptics of the direct primary was Simon.

``Senator Simon is not a great lover of the direct primary law and does not believe that it will do what it was hoped it would,'' the Oregonian reported.

But the Oregonian dismissed Simon's suggestion, declaring: ``The opposition of every machine politician to the primary law is irreconcilable with Mr. Simon's contention that the machine can rule things as effectively now as heretofore.''

Simon's election drew national attention.

``A Hebrew Senator,'' read newspaper headlines.

``Truth Stranger Than Fiction,'' read the headline in the Corvallis Gazette.

Reaction to Simon's election was mixed.

``His election is doubtless one of the greatest political surprises ever,'' the Detroit Journal wrote, calling Simon ``tricky, resourceful and audacious.''

Still, the paper said that while Simon served in the state Senate, ``he distinguished himself as a painstaking and conscientious legislator, much to the surprise of those who anticipated that he would prostitute his office to serve political ends.''

Some were simply relieved that the legislative stalemate was over.

``The agony is over at Salem,'' proclaimed the Hood River Glacier. The Astorian called Simon's election a ``happy termination of a political struggle that has disgraced the state.''

``No Better Could Have Been Chosen,'' read the headline in the Lebanon Criterion.

Simon has been ``the object of more newspaper criticism and abuse than any other politician in the state,'' the Corvallis Gazette noted.

Yet, the paper paid tribute to Simon's political skills, noting that he has "played many daring and even at times desperate games on the political chess board and has seldom met with defeat" and has "secured a valuable and interesting collection of political scalps as trophies of his numerous triumphs."

"No man in Oregon is better qualified from every point of view to represent the state in the United States Senate than Joseph Simon," wrote the Astorian.

"He is an honorable man, an able man, a truthful man, a sincere man. He is not a sectional man, but will look after and serve with even-handed justice the interests of every community in the state.... He will take as much pleasure in doing a real favor for a Democratic or Populist fellow citizen as for one who is a Republican."

Said the Oakland Gazette: "Mr. Simon has been in the Oregon State Senate for 20 years, and therefore possesses a complete knowledge of the state's needs, having labored assiduously down through those years for the expansion of her interests, and for the development of her resources."

And the Lincoln County Leader predicted Simon would make a good senator.

"He is brainy, he is ambitious, he is a worker, he is a good organizer, and he has no peer in our state as a parliamentarian."

Simon was "abused as much as any man who ever mixed in politics in Oregon," the Hood River Glacier wrote.

"But no man was ever abused more unjustly," the paper added.

The Milton Eagle, citing Simon's reputation as political boss, expressed hope that his election to the Senate would reform him, as the Civil War reformed Ulysses S. Grant.

"Grant is now called the great soldier-statesman, yet the writer can remember when he was characterized by his political opponent as a low political mountebank," the paper wrote.

The State Rights Democrat of Albany, Ore., described Simon as a member of the "wire pullers" and "Mark Hanna on a smaller scale," a reference to the Ohio Republican senator and power broker.

"He is so much of a politician," the paper said of Simon, "there is a danger that he will have politics in his eyes in everything."

Sen. Joseph Simon. San Francisco Call, 1898.

The Woodburn Independent lamented that Simon's election amounted to the "oiling of a political machine that will hereafter run the whole state instead of only Portland. It is the creation of a state boss."

The Dalles Times-Mountaineer was brutal in its assessment of the new senator.

"When one compares the gentleman just elected by the Oregon legislature to the United States Senate with some of his predecessors, he must conclude the standard of statesmanship is not advancing," the paper wrote.

"When compared to (former U.S. senators) Joseph N. Dolph and James W. Nesmith, Mr. Simon must suffer. They were statesmen, he is a politician. They were men whose political methods were never questioned; Mr. Simon has been known for years as a political boss and trixter."

The San Francisco Call reported that some of those "who still worship at the shrine of ex-Senator Mitchell" were "sullen and heartsore" over their defeat.

Some newspapers assailed Simon for seeking full pay for lawmakers responsible for the hold-up session.

The lawmakers who participated in the hold-up session not only "rendered no service whatsoever to the state," the Dalles Times-Mountaineer wrote, but "their rebellious action cost the taxpayers of Oregon over $100,000."

The newspaper also complained about the $30,000 cost of convening a special session to elect Simon as U.S. senator and $3,000 to choose his successor to the state Senate.

"Joseph is a pretty expensive luxury to the state and will have to do some pretty good rustling in the Senate if the people get even. Nothing short of the Nicaraguan canal and a big appropriation for opening the Columbia River will compensate for the expense he has put us to."

Simon became the fourth Jewish senator in U.S. history. He was the first Jewish senator outside the South and the first Republican Jewish senator.

The first Jewish senator, David Levy Yulee, was a Democrat elected in 1845 from Florida when the state was admitted to the Union. Yulee resigned from the Senate after Florida seceded from the Union.

He was followed by Judah P. Benjamin, elected as a Whig in 1852 from Louisiana. He later became a Democrat. Benjamin could have been the first Jewish member of the U.S. Supreme Court but declined the appointment, preferring instead to serve in the Senate. Benjamin was so ardently pro-slavery that a fellow senator called him "an Israelite with Egyptian principles." Benjamin resigned from the Senate and was appointed attorney general of the Confederacy by his friend Jefferson Davis. Benjamin later served as the Confederacy's secretary of war and secretary of state.

After Judah P. Benjamin came Benjamin F. Jonas, a Democrat elected in 1879, also from Louisiana.

Simon's Jewish heritage was noted in stories.

"Joseph Simon is the First Northern Jew in the U.S. Senate," read a headline in the Topeka Capital newspaper. During his time in the nation's capital, Simon also was the only Jewish senator.

Simon's election to the Senate "shows the success which any citizen can reach in this country," trumpeted the Jamestown Weekly Alert of North Dakota.

In Philadelphia, Rabbi J.B. Grossman of Beth-Israel synagogue cheered Simon's election as a "notable example of freedom from narrow sectarianism," the Oregonian reported.

Grossman called Simon a "man who never apologized for his Judaism any more than he would for his Americanism."

His election, the rabbi said, provided a "valuable lesson that under our secular form of government, political preferment is open to all citizens regardless of religious belief, and that to gain the highest prizes of political ambition a man need not surrender his religious convictions or forswear his conscience."

Grossman called Simon a "self-made man, starting from humble beginnings, to blaze his way to renown through difficulties and obstacles which would have overwhelmed with discouragement the most ambitious."

"His success is a striking illustration of the conquering force of American 'grit,' when impregnated with the quality known as Hebrew perseverance."

In Oregon, the Rainier Review wrote: "It gives us that tired feeling to hear some papers constantly prating about Joe Simon being a Jew, as if that were a disqualification for United States Senator or any other office. We believe the Constitution does not require a religious test, and it is very poor taste, to say the very least, to harp on that one string.

"Joe Simon is not of our political faith," the paper added. "but it makes no difference to us whether he be a Jew, Pagan or Gentile, if he makes Oregon a good senator. There is one thing about the man that we must all admire; he has always been successful. Nothing succeeds like success."

The Oregon Mist, citing the Rainier Review editorial, remarked: "In the election of Mr. Simon, a man who has never apologized for his Judaism any more than he would for his Americanism, emphasizes the valuable lesson that under our secular form of government political preferment is open to all citizens, regardless of religious belief."

"I hail Simon's coming as a healthy sign of the times," Champ

Clark, the Missourian who later became speaker of the House, wrote. "It demonstrates that the ancient and hereditary prejudice against the Israelites is dying out, as it ought, in this 'land of the free and home of the brave.'"

Even so, Simon occasionally was the subject of anti-Semitic attacks in newspapers.

Perhaps as important, if not more, than Simon's religion was his position on the economic issue of the day.

"My election is really a triumph for the gold standard," Simon told the San Francisco Call while visiting San Francisco a few days after his election.

"Oregon wanted a man who is sound upon the great financial question," the Lebanon Criterion wrote, "and none have been more ardent supporters of sound money than Mr. Simon."

Added the Chicago Tribune: "The most important fact regarding the new senator is that he is a gold-standard man."

At the time, the country—and Simon's Republican party – were deeply divided by "gold bugs," led by bankers and businessmen who favored a gold standard, and "silverites," led by farmers and laborers who supported gold and silver or bimetallism. The money debate was an emotional issue in the 1896 presidential election, which followed a financial panic in 1893.

"Sound money" men like Simon—and Republican presidential candidate William McKinley—contended that a tighter money supply through the gold standard would provide greater economic stability. "Free silver" advocates like Democratic presidential candidate William Jennings Bryan argued that a more flexible currency would put more money in the hands of workers and ease the nation's economic troubles.

"The whole nation has reason to be thankful" that the Oregon legislature chose Simon, a firm supporter of the gold standard, to succeed Mitchell, a wobbler on the money question, the Milwaukee-based Weekly Wisconsin wrote.

Congress in 1900, with Simon's support, approved the Gold Standard Act.

McKinley used a gold pen to sign to the legislation.

CHAPTER FIVE

The first Jewish Republican senator arrives in Washington

When Simon arrived in the nation's capital, William McKinley was president, Republicans controlled Congress, and the Senate had 90 members – all men.

Senators were paid $5,000 a year (the current annual salary is $174,000).

Brass spittoons adorned the Senate chamber (a few remain but are purely decorative). There was no air conditioning (it would be installed in 1929).

The Washington Monument towered over the city, but the Lincoln Memorial had yet to be built. (It would be dedicated in 1922). The Supreme Court resided in the Capitol. (It got its own building in 1935). Congress included Civil War veterans.

Oregon's new senator most likely arrived at the Baltimore and Potomac train station, site of President James A. Garfield's assassination in 1881.

A star on the floor marked the spot of the shooting. But it was removed in 1897 after complaints from travelers who didn't want to be reminded of the crime every time they walked through the station, the New York Times reported. The depot was demolished after Union Station opened in 1907.

The trip from Oregon to Washington, D.C. took several days. While the travel was long by today's standards, it wasn't insufferable. The train featured a sleeping car, dining car, library and barber. But train robberies were still a threat.

As Simon was making his way to Washington, representatives of Spain and the United States were in Paris preparing to sign the treaty ending the Spanish-American War. Spain ceded Guam and Puerto Rico to the United States, renounced all claims to Cuba and sold the Philippines to the U.S. for $20 million.

Weighing in on a fiery political issue of the day, Simon told newspapers that he favored keeping the Philippines and all other conquered territory, calling them "legitimate fruits of war."

Simon was an "imperialist in the full application of the word," wrote the Independent newspaper. The Fargo, N.D., Daily Argus called the new senator "as progressive on the subject of expansion and manifest destiny as Admiral Dewey."

There was a belief that expanding Uncle Sam's footprint in the world would strengthen the nation's defenses against foreign attack and open new markets for U.S. goods. The contrary view was that it was wrong for the United States, which rebelled from colonial rule, to seek to force it on others.

Simon's belief was that "the American people would never sanction the surrender of a foot of ground won by our army in the Far East," the Lewiston Daily Teller of Idaho reported.

The New York Times assailed Simon's remarks "on the ground that a senator is bound, in matters of great importance, to inform his judgment not only by study but by the debate that is sure to arise in the Senate before reaching a definitive conclusion.

".... Surely it is not worthwhile for a single senator, freshly elected, without experience in the National Council, and who will exercise only one-ninetieth part of the share the Senate has in making treaties, to decide upon a course he will obstinately follow, no matter what may happen, or what facts and argument may be presented by the President or by his fellow senators," the New York Times wrote.

Some newspapers, however, praised Simon's straightforwardness.

"Senator Simon makes a good first impression by his frank avowal of generally sound views," the Wilkes-Barre Record of Pennsylvania wrote.

It must have been sweet for Simon to read the Wilkes-Barre newspaper call him "a decided improvement on his predecessor, John

Hipple Mitchell, who at best was only a politician, constantly trimming his sails to catch what he supposed to be popular breezes."

Simon "not only has convictions, but is not in the least afraid to say what they are," the Milwaukee Sentinel wrote.

When Simon stepped foot in the Senate chamber to take the oath of office on Dec. 5, 1898, the odor of burning wood in fireplaces filled the air.

The galleries were packed for the opening day of the session.

The chamber was decorated with flowers, "so thickly strewn over desks that the dignified statesmen who sat behind them had to step out in the aisle to be seen," the Washington Evening Times reported.

Oregon Sen. John McBride, a Republican, presented his junior colleague's credentials as Simon took the oath of office from Vice President Garrett Hobart. The next day, Simon visited President McKinley at the Executive Mansion.

The Senate clerk read the president's message, taking 2 hours and 18 minutes. "As is usual, little attention was given to the presentation of the message, either in the galleries or on the floor, after the first few pages," reported the Oregon City Courier-Herald.

There was one hitch to Simon's first day in the Senate: there was no place for him to sit on the Republican side of the chamber.

"The new senator resented the suggestion that he sit on the Democratic side," the Los Angeles Herald reported. The snafu was blamed on the fact that one of Oregon's Senate seats had been vacant for more than a year and a half.

It was an inauspicious way for the freshman senator to gain nationwide attention, as newspapers throughout the country picked up the story.

"Simon is Seatless," read the Los Angeles Herald headline.

"The New Oregon Senator Had to Stand the First Day," wrote the Dalles Times-Mountaineer.

Simon could not find a seat, the Astorian newspaper joked, because his long-time nemesis, former Senator John H. Mitchell, "brought it back to Oregon with him."

Soon, Simon was seated at the end of the last row of the chamber. In 1901, he moved up to a coveted front-row seat to the left of the presiding officer after Senate retirements.

Lacking a seat was the least of Simon's problems.

The freshman senator faced a daunting task of trying to get along with fellow senators after engineering the defeat of the popular Mitchell. Simon, a political power in Oregon, also had to adjust to being in a chamber full of senators who wielded political power in their own right.

Still, the new senator drew attention.

``A little man is Simon,'' the Washington Post reported, ``being scarcely as tall as the legs of Fairbanks are long,'' a reference to 6-foot-4 Sen. Charles Fairbanks (R-Ind.).

Idaho Gov. Frank Steunenberg said he was surprised when he met Simon.

``I had expected to see a man six-feet-three and as big around as a tree,'' he said, the Oregonian reported. ``I could scarcely believe my eyes when I saw him. I had so often heard of Joe Simon and his work that I had come to look upon him as a heavyweight in size as well as in politics.''

As for Simon's height, the Eugene City Guard remarked, ``Joe Simon's political dimensions are not to be measured by his physical proportions.''

Newspaper coverage of Simon's diminutive stature prompted the home-state Daily Journal of Salem to call attention to another of the senator's attributes: ``He is as tough as they make them…And he has a backbone like a steel rail.''

The freshman Simon shocked Senate colleagues upon his arrival by expecting to win plum committee assignments.

``Senators are enjoying themselves at the expense of their new colleague,'' newspapers reported, noting that Simon was seeking to be placed on one of the Senate's most important committees.

``A senator speaking of him said: `Simon is a peach. He beats anything we have had here for some time. Just think of it, before he had been in the Senate for 24 hours, he filed an application for a position on the Committee on Rules.''

Newspapers ridiculed Simon for seeking a seat on the powerful Rules Committee ``before he had been here long enough to know how to make a motion to adjourn.'' Veteran Republican Senator Nelson Aldrich ``nearly had a fit when Simon made his wishes known to him,'' newspapers wrote.

Newspapers joked that the ambitious Simon had a good chance of landing a seat on the ``Committee to Look after Ventilation in the Interior Department.''

What plum committee assignments did Simon finally receive?

The Committee to Investigate the Condition of the Potomac River Front at Washington was one.

Sen. Robert M. La Follette (R-Wis.) wrote in his autobiography that when he was named chairman of the Potomac River panel in 1906, "I had immediate visions of cleaning up the whole Potomac River front. Then I found that in all its history, the committee had never had a bill referred to it for consideration, and had never held a meeting."

Simon also was tapped for a seat on the Committee on Revolutionary War Claims, with little to do 115 years after the war's conclusion. He also was assigned to the Select Committee to Investigate Trespassers Upon Indian Lands.

Later, Simon snagged a seat on the Judiciary Committee, a hotbed for debate on anti-trust legislation. He also served on the Pensions Committee, including chairing an investigation into charges that a presidential nominee for a federal position had shot an unarmed prisoner in cold blood while serving in the U.S. military in the Philippines. The nominee was cleared of wrongdoing.

Simon was singled out in an article in the Mitchell, S.D., Capital newspaper as among the senators "who listen with the greatest attention, who are rarely absent from the seats and who read the bills and study the reports and give more time to general legislation than all others."

Simon occasionally presided over the Senate, performing a task occasionally carried out—unenthusiastically—by Vice President Theodore Roosevelt.

Shortly after his election to the Senate, Simon attended a sensational trial in New York City.

Fayne Strahan Moore, daughter of one of Simon's former law partners, and her husband were accused of attempting to extort $50,000 from a wealthy New York hotel owner. Newspapers called it the "notorious Badger Game trial."

The married hotel owner testified that he was lured to Mrs. Moore's room by the charming, younger woman. While he was "in a compromising position," her husband broke in and demanded money.

"The trial was the sensation of the decade," the Ogden Standard reported.

The Pittsburgh Daily Post reported a "wild scramble for seats when the doors of the courtroom opened." Six policemen fought the crowd at the door, the paper added.

The case, featuring what one newspaper headlined "spicy testimony," was so scandalous that "the testimony was unfit for publication."

William A.E. Moore was sentenced to 19 years in Sing Sing Prison, while his wife went free.

"One juryman, interviewed after she was acquitted, declared that no judge or jury in the world would believe anything ill of such a wide-eyed, innocent looking girl," the Ogden Standard reported.

As Senator Simon was settling into his new home, the nation's capital was hit by the coldest temperature ever recorded there– minus 15 degrees – and nearly three feet of snow in what became known as the Great Blizzard of 1899.

"Blasts that would have chilled a polar bear blew through the city," the Washington Times reported. The New York Times wrote that the U.S. Capitol looked like a "snow palace."

"In the Washington monument grounds, the snow has piled up in some places in drifts ten and twelve feet deep," the Washington Star reported. Congress moved quickly to provide funds to clear ice from the Potomac River and snow from the streets after officials warned it would be difficult for fire engines to reach fires and trucks to deliver coal and other necessities to homes.

In his first address on the Senate floor, Simon presented a resolution from the Oregon Legislature urging Congress to approve the peace treaty between Spain and the United States.

The treaty was ratified by the Senate, 57-27, one vote more than the two thirds necessary.

Simon joined most of his Republican colleagues in responding "aye" when his name was called.

The treaty was one of a number of measures that came before Simon dealing with America's expanding influence in the world.

Simon voted in 1901 for a measure opening the door to the U.S. naval base at Cuba's Guantanamo Bay. The legislation established the terms under which the United States would end its military occupation of Cuba, including requiring the leasing of land for a U.S. naval base. The base, sometimes referred to as Gitmo, is still in use.

Simon was an enthusiastic supporter of a canal connecting the Atlantic and Pacific oceans.

``You will find few people in the West who do not heartily favor the building of the canal,'' he told the Oregonian in 1900. ``The (Pacific) coast will reap great benefits from it.''

Simon favored Nicaragua for the canal route but was okay with Panama. (In a bit of creative lobbying before a key vote, promoters of the Panama route sent each senator a postage stamp picturing a smoking volcano in Nicaragua as evidence of the danger of building the canal there.)

When the Senate voted on a canal bill, the St. Paul Globe trumpeted it in a headline: ``Big Ditch Across the Isthmus To Be Dug by the American Government.''

Simon was in the Senate when it ratified a treaty providing for U.S. purchase of the Danish West Indies for $5 million, though it would take another treaty—and payment of $25 million—to close the deal before the United States would acquire the islands of St. Thomas, St. John and St. Croix, known today as the U.S. Virgin Islands. During Simon's term, the Senate also ratified a treaty paving the way for the eastern islands of Samoa to come under U.S. control.

Simon saw a robust role for the United States in world affairs.

``While I do not believe in the jingo policy, I am still averse to our withdrawing within our national shell and refusing to take and hold our proper place in the affairs of the world,'' he told the Oregonian. ``We cannot keep aloof of the world's great activities without suffering the penalty.''

In 1899, Simon was among a group of ``men of national reputation,'' as the New York World put it, who signed a ``peace petition'' urging President McKinley to offer the United States as a mediator in the Boer War.

Simon wrestled with issues that are still hotly debated today: immigration, trade, government regulation and federal spending.

Among his priorities: enlarging the Army to 100,000 soldiers and strengthening the Navy.

``While we hope to maintain peaceable relations with the world, we should not be at the mercy of any nation at any time," he told the Oregonian.

He understood the adage "All politics is local" long before it was uttered in the nation's capital.

Simon pushed for funding for Oregon's rivers and harbors and War Department purchase of cavalry horses from Oregon. He successfully lobbied Secretary of War Elihu Root to make Portland a departure point for sending U.S. troops and supplies to the Philippines. He worked to ensure that stone from Oregon, not another state, was used in building a new Salem courthouse.

He also supported legislation providing pensions to aging veterans of Indian wars, including wars in Oregon in the 1850s.

"Veterans of the Fifties Receive Justice At Last," read the Oregon Statesman Journal headline following passage of the bill in 1902. The measure, a priority of the Oregon congressional delegation, provided payments of $8 a month to the veterans or their survivors.

Even then, advocates saw a benefit to putting a personal face to their cause. Several Indian war veterans from Oregon traveled to Washington to lobby for the pensions. Among them was a 77-year-old veteran who "still carries an arrow head in his hip" received in battle in 1848, the Washington Post reported.

Among the issues Simon faced in the hallowed marble halls of Congress: prunes.

Oregon agricultural officials asked Simon to oppose a treaty with France that would reduce tariffs on prunes, warning it could spell disaster for the state's prune industry.

Among the Simon bills signed into law was a measure extending to California, Oregon and Washington residents a law that permitted the cutting of timber from public mineral lands for use in building, agriculture and mining.

Shortly after Simon arrived in the Senate, the powerful Senator Mark Hanna (R-Ohio) took him under his wing, newspapers reported.

Kentucky Sen. William Deboe and Simon had seats near Hanna and "confer with him on knotty points of constitutional law and other matters," the paper reported. And, "they follow Hanna's lead in voting."

The New York World called Simon Hanna's new protégé.

"Senator Simon and Senator Hanna are great friends," the paper wrote, "and because of the fact that Senator Hanna is one of the powers in the Senate, Simon believes Hanna is a pretty good man to tie to."

Simon, nonetheless, opposed a shipbuilding subsidy championed by Hanna.

In a letter to a constituent published in the Salem Journal, Simon said, "I cannot conceive why this government should pay these proposed large subsidies to a lot of wealthy shipowners."

The paper praised his stand with a headline: "Making a Record in the Senate that an Independent Might be Proud of." The ship subsidy bill, nonetheless, passed the Senate.

Simon, an advocate of free trade, also broke from most of his Republican colleagues to oppose tariffs on goods shipped between Puerto Rico and the continental United States.

Simon expressed regret for breaking from "so many of my party" but noted that his position was in accord with the "overwhelming sentiment of the people of my state."

During the 1900 debate, Simon assailed the tariffs—-which effectively treated Puerto Rico as a foreign country—as discriminatory and "unjust to the people of Puerto Rico, and in violation of the promises made to them."

When U.S. forces occupied the island, Puerto Ricans were promised "the same rights, the same privileges, the same immunities and the same benefits" as Americans, Simon told colleagues.

"If we cannot afford to permit Puerto Rico to have free commercial intercourse with the rest of the country, it is high time for us to declare that we are incapable of either governing or protecting that island, and we should haul down our flag and abandon our efforts to do either," he said.

He called the tariff legislation a "serious party blunder" for Republicans, warning it could cost McKinley support in the next presidential election.

Among the tariff's supporters, Sen. Chauncey Depew (R-N.Y.) argued it would generate money to support Puerto Rico, "for their schoolhouses, for their roads, for the relief of their starving," and suggested that without the tariff, U.S. taxpayers would be on the hook to support the island.

The bill, which also established a civilian government for Puerto Rico, passed the Senate, 40-31, with Simon voting no.

Newspapers lauded the senator for his courage in bucking party leaders.

``Senator Simon has had the nerve to differ with his party," the Journal in Salem wrote, citing Simon's defiance of party leaders in opposing the Puerto Rico tariff and shipbuilding subsidy bills.

``Oh, for another Simon in the Senate from this state, and Oregon would regain her lost prestige in that body," the Antelope Valley Herald, an Oregon newspaper, wrote.

The Baltimore Sun wrote that Simon and the other Republican senators who broke from their party to vote no ``deserve to have their names written high on the roster of justice and fairness."

Wrote the Elgin Recorder, an Oregon newspaper: ``While the election of Joe Simon to the United States Senate lacked a whole lot of being satisfactory to all the Republicans of Oregon, he is nevertheless proving himself a statesman of more than ordinary ability. Unlike his colleague, Mr. McBride, he possesses sufficient independence to go contrary to the majority of his party when it goes contrary to what he considers right."

``For a senator who is not expected to have any mind of his own, Simon is a stupendous failure," the Capital Journal wrote. ``He knows he has nothing to gain from following in the footsteps of politicians who rely on plunder more than upon principle as the basis for their attitude upon important public questions."

``The Times-Mountaineer has ordinarily been opposed to Little Joe Simon," the paper wrote, ``but now must acknowledge that he is a bigger man than it had ever thought him to be."

``Notwithstanding he is a political boss, and we believe an unscrupulous politician, he is a patriot, and we honor him," the paper added.

The Oregonian called Simon's vote a ``remarkable and praiseworthy exhibition of political courage and loyalty to the conscience and the welfare of the people of Oregon and the entire Pacific Coast."

And in a sort of backhanded compliment, the State Rights Democrat of Albany, Ore., wrote that if Simon stands firm in his opposition to the tariff, ```we will forgive him for some of his past crookedness."

"If Joe Simon, Oregon's senator, keeps on," the paper added, citing his breaks from his party, "he will be a first-class Democrat."

"Subsidy or no subsidy the shipyards are all busy and the business is very profitable," editorialized the Daily Journal of Salem, Ore. "Senator Simon of Oregon is one man who has no use for the subsidy swindle, that would tax a thousand farmers to enrich one ship owner. Watch Mark Hanna's army of chipmunk politicians fight Simon for having a mind of his own."

Said the Albany Democrat: "Papers of all politics throughout the state seem to be against Simon, and yet as a matter of fact Simon has come nearer voting right on important questions than most any senator Oregon has had for many years, regardless of his wire pulling methods in local politics."

Simon witnessed historic events during his time in Washington.

He was likely present for an 1899 homecoming celebration for Admiral George Dewey, following his stunning victory in the Battle of Manila Bay. Dewey was presented a jeweled sword by President McKinley before a cheering crowd at the Capitol. Congress also voted to elevate Dewey to admiral of the Navy, the only officer to ever hold the rank.

Women's suffrage was a hot issue during Simon's time in the Senate. Susan B. Anthony led suffragists to a Senate hearing in 1900, but it's not known whether Simon swung by the room to catch a glimpse of the celebrated suffragist.

Oregon women won the right to vote in 1914. Simon was out of the Senate when Congress in 1919 approved the women's suffrage amendment and sent it to the states for ratification. But when Simon was in the Oregon Legislature, he voted in 1895 against a constitutional amendment giving women the right to vote.

Simon in 1899 did support the creation of a museum in Washington to recognize women's contributions.

"The time has arrived when our women should be remembered by a paternal government," says a booklet prepared by proponents of the Woman's National Industrial Exhibit. "Our public parks are graced by the statues of generals, admirals and statesmen, while woman is relegated to obscurity, with not a dollar appropriated to celebrate her worth." (Frances Willard, a pioneer in the temperance movement, became the first woman to be honored with a statue in the U.S. Capitol's Statuary Hall in 1905. Women, however, remain underrepresented among the statues in the nation's capital.)

Working conditions were an issue during Simon's Senate term.

Simon joined the overwhelming majority of his Republican colleagues in preventing a vote in 1900 on an eight-hour work week, despite an appeal by labor leader Samuel Gompers. Simon's business allies opposed federal regulation of work hours. (Congress in 1916 voted to require an eight-hour workday and overtime pay for railroad workers. But the issue would continue to be debated until President Franklin D. Roosevelt in 1938 signed the Fair Labor Standards Act establishing a maximum work week of 44 hours and, two years later, 40 hours.)

Simon also was confronted with Teddy Roosevelt's trust-busting legislation.

He supported the creation of the Department of Commerce and Labor, which included a Bureau of Corporations with the power to investigate trusts. (The New York Sun, reporting on the prospects of anti-trust legislation in 1903, noted Simon hailed from a state "where octopus hunting is a very popular pastime." The octopus was a reference to monopolies with their many tentacles holding onto different industries).

Simon supported railroad regulation, including a measure outlawing rebates and authorizing stiff fines on railroads for offering rebates and on shippers for accepting rebates.

The Elkins Act, named after its chief sponsor, Sen. Stephen Elkins (R-W.Va.), grew out of concern that companies receiving often secretive rebates gained a competitive advantage.

It might come as a surprise that Simon, an old railroad attorney, would favor increased regulation of the industry.

But the legislation was supported by many railroads—-and supposedly drafted by the president of the Pennsylvania Railroad—which hated having to pay rebates to high-volume shippers in order to hold onto their business.

The bill, which won unanimous Senate approval, was "the child of the railroads themselves," wrote the Missouri-based Macon Times-Democrat, because "it will save the railroads much money."

But Simon also supported railroad safety legislation, even though it was opposed by the industry due to its cost. The legislation was pushed by railroad workers who said it would reduce deaths and injuries.

Simon, in spite of his strong ties to business, supported legislation to prevent abuses by trusts.

Simon called for the 1900 national Republican platform to declare that "the formation of immense combinations of capital for controlling the products and prices of commodities in the United States should be declared a violation of sound economic doctrine," according to the Oregonian.

Simon broke from most of his Republican colleagues to support regulation to better protect the public from tainted food and drugs.

His support for a federal pure food law was not surprising, given that the law was sought by businesses.

"The legitimate producer or manufacturer of honest goods is as much interested in the suppression of frauds as is the consumer," wrote the San Francisco Call newspaper. The Oregon legislature passed a resolution citing the "serious menace" to public health from adulterated and mislabeled food. The Farmers' Congress of Oregon also expressed support for a national pure food law.

About a year before the bill came before the Senate, the U.S. Agriculture Department's chief chemist W.H. Wiley appeared before a congressional committee with a "sample of so-called wine, made, he said, from alcohol, sugar, and coal tar, with no product of the vine," the Washington Post reported.

But the Senate refused to take up the bill. Opponents argued that regulation was best left to states, an argument that is still made today in opposition to federal regulation. In 1906, however, President Roosevelt signed the Pure Food and Drugs Act.

Simon was on hand for 1902 Senate passage of the Virus Act, or Biologics Control Act, the first federal drug safety regulation. Congress passed the measure after children died from contaminated diphtheria antitoxin and smallpox vaccine.

Simon was in the Senate when Congress in 1899 voted to create Mount Rainier National Park in Washington state as the nation's fifth national park.

Simon's support for the park probably wasn't rooted in his love for the outdoors or conservationist John Muir's appeals to preserve the area. Simon's railroad friends saw national parks as a way to boost business by drawing railroad-riding visitors to the West.

Oregon's only national park -- Crater Lake National Park -- was created during Simon's time in the Senate. The park's creation in 1902 followed years of debate and came only after conservationist President Roosevelt helped muscle the bill through Congress.

Simon supported other conservation measures, including voting to preserve a spectacular grove of giant sequoias after the big trees came under threat from the "woodman's ax."

He was in the Senate for the 1900 passage of the nation's first federal wildlife protection measure. The Lacey Act, named after Congressman John Lacey of Iowa and originally enacted to prevent the interstate shipment of game killed in violation of state and local laws, has been strengthened over the years and remains a powerful wildlife protection tool.

Nearly four decades after the Civil War ended, Simon and his Senate colleagues were still dealing with war-related legislation.

Simon was in the Senate when Congress in 1902 approved a measure providing payments to former Confederate soldiers, or their survivors, for horses, saddles, side arms and other property taken after the war ended in violation of the terms of the surrender.

"General Grant is said to have remarked that the men 'would need their horses for spring plowing,' and he could hardly have expected them to ride home bareback and without bridles," the Indianapolis Journal wrote in reporting on the legislation.

Simon voted to confirm President Roosevelt's nomination of Oliver Wendell Holmes to the Supreme Court.

The Prohibition movement dogged Simon during his days in Washington, as it did during his time in Oregon. This was the era of Carrie Nation, famous for wielding a hatchet against saloons.

The Woman's Christian Temperance Union declared at its 1898 Oregon convention that the state had a right to exclude as a nuisance "anything which affects deleteriously the physical or moral well-being of the citizen, be that a cesspool, a pigpen, or a saloon."

Simon, though an opponent of Prohibition, voted to ban alcohol sales at Army canteens.

``No Beer for the Nation's Defenders,'' read the New York Times headline.

The ban was pushed by churches and temperance groups, including Portland's Ministerial Association. Shortly after its enactment, the Association of Military Surgeons urged Congress to repeal the ban, warning that it would lead to an increase in ``intemperance, insubordination, discontent, desertion, and disease'' in the Army. The acting Secretary of War also warned that the ban would drive enlisted men to leave Army posts and ``drink bad whiskey to excess.''

Simon received petitions from the Woman's Christian Temperance Union to ban alcohol in other places, including new U.S. territories. But an effort to prohibit the importation or sale of distilled spirits into the Philippines, ``except for medicinal purposes,'' was defeated in the Senate, with Simon voting no.

Congress, during Simon's times, also voted to prohibit the sale of intoxicants inside the Capitol.

Praising the decision, the Evening Times-Republican, an Iowa newspaper, noted: ``Leaders in national affairs have participated in incidents as a result of generous libations at the Capitol bar that would have brought upon them a storm of indignant reproof from their constituents and the public if the facts had been printed.''

Newspapers wrote that the ban on alcohol sales in the House restaurant would pose a hardship only on visitors to the Capitol, noting lawmakers would find other ways to imbibe.

``There is, perhaps, not a committee room on the Senate side in which a private bottle may not be found,'' the Washington Post reported.

During Simon's tenure in the Senate, Congress passed legislation limiting building heights in the nation's capital, a measure that has helped to preserve the grand views of the Capitol, the Washington Monument and other majestic landmarks. Congress also authorized building of Washington's Union Station, still in use.

Among the bills passed during his tenure in the Senate: ``An act for the suppression of train robbery.'' Also approved was a measure that authorized the use of voting machines in federal elections.

Bills introduced by Simon included a measure to establish a laboratory in the Justice Department for the study of the ``criminal, pauper and defective classes.''

Simon spent a good deal of time dealing with correspondence (at the time, senators were assigned one clerk) and sending out packages of seeds to constituents.

That's right. Seeds!

For decades, members of Congress received thousands of packets of free seeds for distribution to constituents. The program was so popular among senators that the Senate in 1901 voted to increase funding for the seeds, from $170,000 to $270,000. Simon was absent for the vote.

The politically popular program, begun as a way to promote agriculture, was attacked as a scheme for lawmakers to sow goodwill among voters. ``Some congressmen may distribute free onion seeds in the joyous hope of being in good odor with their constituents,'' the Daily Astorian sniffed.

Congress ended the program in 1923.

Among the more entertaining moments for Simon during his Senate days was his involvement in the 1900 commemoration of the centennial of Washington, D.C.'s founding as the nation's capital.

As a member of the Committee on the Centennial Celebration of the Establishment of the Seat of Government in the District of Columbia, he was likely on hand for the ceremonies, including a military parade down Pennsylvania Avenue.

Simon attended McKinley's second inauguration in the cold rain on the east portico of the U.S. Capitol in 1901.

Six months later, McKinley was assassinated by a professed anarchist at the Pan-American Exposition in Buffalo, N.Y. Simon was among a group of lawmakers who advocated a law ``directed toward the extinction of anarchy in the United States,'' according to the Washington Star.

In 1903, Congress passed and President Roosevelt signed the Anarchist Exclusion Act to prohibit entry and allow deportation of ``anarchists, or persons who believe in or advocate the overthrow by force or violence of the Government of the United States.... or the assassination of public officials.''

Simon was among 20,000 mourners who attended a Portland tribute to the slain president. "Never in the history of Portland has business been so generally suspended as it was yesterday," the Oregonian reported. "Even the saloons were closed, and a drink could not be had for love or money."

Simon weighed in on the news of the day, including the Dreyfus affair.

He was reported as outraged by France's treatment of Capt. Alfred Dreyfus, the Jewish army officer wrongly convicted of treason. But Simon balked at the suggestion that the United States withdraw from the 1900 Paris Exposition in protest.

"He thinks the government has proceeded so far that it cannot withdraw, and furthermore that because of an injustice to an individual or even a class, it might not be proper for a government, as a government, to lay itself open to international complications," the Oregonian reported.

"But for the people of this country, especially all Jews, the senator says their duty is to resent the outrage in every way possible, particularly in boycotting the fair to the limit of their ability."

Simon said he favored boycotting the fair "as an expression of the world's contempt and disapproval of the course adopted by France.... I believe it is a farce, a travesty of justice."

As a prominent official, Simon was naturally asked his opinion about a wide range of matters.

But one of the more bizarre topics dealt with claims by Dr. William Osler, a founding professor of medicine at Johns Hopkins University, declaring that men became less effective at age 40, and at 60, became so useless they should be retired "or chloroformed." Some said that Osler's advocacy of chloroform was a joke, but that he did believe that men over 60 were useless.

Simon called the claims "foolish and absurd."

"My personal observation has been decidedly to the contrary," Simon told the Oregonian in 1905. "I believe a great number, in fact the majority of men, accomplish more after they have passed their fortieth year than before."

Simon's name was invoked during a 1903 sermon by the Rev. Robert S. MacArthur at New York City's Cavalry Baptist Church condemning Russia for prohibiting American Jews with valid passports from visiting.

"It is a striking fact that the Russian consul in New York conducts a tribunal to ascertain the faith of American citizens who apply to him for an endorsement of their passports, and when he discovers that an American citizen is a Jew, he dishonors our government's certificate of citizenship," MacArthur said, according to a New York Times story.

"If there were a convention of statesmen (in Russia), President Roosevelt and Gov. Odell would be admitted, but Mr. Simon of Oregon and our noble fellow citizen Oscar S. Straus, who so ably represented us as minister to Turkey, would be rejected."

He ended up with a spiffy Capitol Hill office after he became chairman of the Committee on Irrigation and Reclamation of Arid Lands in the 56th and 57th Congresses.

The office looked out on the botanical gardens and the "big park stretching to the Potomac river and looking out upon the broad street, Pennsylvania Avenue, where all parades of national importance take place," the Oregonian reported in 1889.

But while Simon enjoyed an office with a spectacular view of Washington, he drew criticism for his lack of leadership on irrigation issues.

A story in the Great Falls Tribune said Simon, as chairman, seemed to take a "perfunctory" interest in the matters that came before the committee.

A landmark irrigation bill passed Congress in 1902, but was championed by Francis G. Newlands, a Democratic congressman from Nevada.

The Washington Times called the Reclamation Act of "far-reaching importance." It established the Reclamation Service, which became the Bureau of Reclamation, and provided for the proceeds of federal land sales in the West to go to building dams and other reclamation projects. The legislation was instrumental in promoting agricultural production and the economic growth of Western states.

During his time in the Senate, Simon was assailed by the Arizona Republican newspaper for opposing Arizona statehood in 1903. The paper called it surprising to find the Oregon senator "voting against western interests" in a test vote.

A bill providing for admission of Arizona, New Mexico and Oklahoma into the Union as states passed the House. But it faced trouble in the Republican-controlled Senate, even though the party's 1900 national platform endorsed statehood.

Some Republicans were worried that the new states would vote Democratic and weaken their party's strength in Washington.

"The admission of new states has always been a matter of politics," wrote the Houston Post. The Denver Republican newspaper called it "bad policy" for Republicans to oppose statehood inasmuch as Oklahoma and New Mexico "can be counted on as practically certain" for the Republican column.

One idea floated during the debate was admitting Arizona and New Mexico as one state known as Montezuma. Eventually, Oklahoma was admitted to the Union in 1907, followed by Arizona and New Mexico in 1912.

Among the bills that came before Simon was extension of the Chinese Exclusion Act, first passed in 1882. The law barred Chinese laborers from entering the country and denied U.S. citizenship to Chinese immigrants already here.

The law was repealed in 1943 after China became a U.S. ally in World War. Congress decades later apologized for passing the discriminatory measure.

But in the late 19th and early 20th centuries, lawmakers were under pressure to restrict Chinese immigration.

"'Keep Out Chinese," screamed an Oregonian headline.

A petition seeking extension of the Chinese Exclusion Act was signed by 20,000 Portlanders and presented to Simon.

U.S. workers were among those pushing for continued exclusion citing the threat to their jobs from "cheap labor."

"The day was when we needed cheap labor in the building of railroads and the opening up of the resources of this country," Portland Mayor H.S. Rowe said in 1901. "That we have done, and we no longer need it."

Simon's Oregon Senate colleague, Mitchell, warned fellow Republican senators that failure to pass a strong Chinese exclusion bill would cost the GOP dearly on the Pacific Coast.

In 1902, Simon joined his colleagues on both sides of the aisle in voting to extend the exclusion act, 76-1, with Sen. George F. Hoar

(R-Mass.) casting the lone dissenting vote. The bill was signed into law by Roosevelt.

Simon was in the Senate when a fistfight broke out in the chamber between South Carolina's senators.

``Fisticuffs in the Senate,'' read the headline in Missouri's Iron County Register.

Sen. Benjamin ``Pitchfork Ben'' Tillman accused fellow Democratic Sen. John McLaurin of succumbing to ``improper influences'' to support the treaty ending the Spanish-American War.

McLaurin, who rushed into the chamber after receiving word of the charge, accused Tillman of a ``willful, malicious, and deliberate lie.''

Tillman, sitting near McLaurin, sprung from his seat and hit his South Carolina colleague in the head. McLaurin struck back, punching Tillman in the nose and drawing blood.

Other senators and the Senate sergeant-at-arms rushed to separate the combatants.

After order was restored, Simon joined his colleagues in voting to hold the senators in contempt of the Senate. Some thought Tillman, who threw the first blow, should receive stiffer punishment than McLaurin, who used ``unparliamentary'' language. In the end, the Senate censured both men for their ``disorderly behavior and flagrant violation'' of the rules of decorum.

The fight led to a rule that survives today: ``No senator in debate shall, directly or indirectly, by any form of words impute to another senator or to other senators any conduct or motive unworthy or unbecoming of a senator.''

But just a few months later, Senator Joseph Bailey (D-Texas) created a sensation by grabbing Senator Albert J. Beveridge (R-Ind.) by the throat after a heated debate. Bailey was pulled away by other senators before he could do any harm.

Simon managed to stay above the fray during his time in the Senate, perhaps because he rarely delivered speeches on the Senate floor.

He maintained such a low profile that when he sought to be recognized by the Senate's presiding officer about a month into his term, Senate President Pro Tem William Frye (R-Maine) asked, ``Who is it?''

Frye got to know Simon, often calling upon him to preside over the Senate.

Frye found Simon to be a skillful parliamentarian.

``He ought to be, for he was president of the Oregon Senate for a number of years and knows the methods of procedure thoroughly,'' the Cheyenne Daily Leader reported.

Speaker of the House David B. Henderson said he thought Simon was a ``Presbyterian deacon'' because ``he looked so sober and thoughtful.''

Simon was known as ``the silent man of the Senate,'' the Washington Times reported.

``He is always in his seat when the Senate is in session and spends his time in reading and writing,'' the paper wrote. ``He seldom chats with other senators.''

But when Simon delivered a speech in 1900, it stirred up a hornet's nest.

The Senate was debating whether to seat Matthew S. Quay, who was appointed to a Pennsylvania Senate seat by the governor after the legislature failed to act.

Senator Thomas Carter of Montana, who favored seating Quay, brought up the Oregon governor's appointment of Corbett to the Senate.

Carter explained that he voted against seating Corbett because Corbett was a prime mover behind his state's legislative deadlock and should not be rewarded for his political mischief.

``A large number of senators voted against Mr. Corbett because his appointment was regarded as the culmination of a conspiracy against the government of his state,'' Carter declared.

Those were fighting words to Simon, who knew more about Oregon's 1897 holdup session than any other man in Washington.

Simon declared that he could not permit Carter's ``unjust and untrue charge'' to go unchallenged.

``I speak from personal knowledge of the matter,'' Simon told his colleagues.

Oregon's legislative deadlock was due to ex-Senator Mitchell and to him alone, Simon said.

Mitchell, he said, waffled on whether he would continue to be an "ardent advocate of the free coinage of silver" or embrace the national Republican platform in support of the gold standard.

As a result, Mitchell lost not only the support of Silver Republicans, Democrats and Populists, all of whom supported free silver, but also gold-standard Republicans.

"Neither the advocates of free silver nor the advocates of the gold standard were satisfied," Simon said, "and Mr. Mitchell, seeking to ride two horses, fell between them and was lost."

Simon took a shot at the Montana senator for attempting to cast Oregon as a den of corruption.

The "views of the distinguished senator may have been warped" by corruption in his own state, Simon said. Montana Senator William A. Clark, a copper mining czar, was forced to resign from the Senate in 1900 after being accused of passing out envelopes of cash to members of his state's legislature to win the Senate seat. Shortly thereafter, he regained the seat.

Simon argued that it would be wrong for the Senate to seat Quay after refusing to seat Corbett.

"If we are now to seat Mr. Quay," Simon said, "how will it be possible for the Senate to atone for the great wrong done Mr. Corbett?"

It was a courageous stand for Simon, given that Quay was a powerful political boss, a former Republican National Committee chairman and an ex-senator with plenty of friends in Washington.

A month later, the Senate, by a single vote, refused to seat Quay. Two years later, the Pennsylvania Legislature returned Quay to the U.S. Senate, creating what must have been an awkward, if not chilly, relationship between the Oregon and Pennsylvania Republican bosses.

Simon's speech drew national attention.

"Simon Made A Hit," the Oregonian declared in a front-page headline. The paper reported that Simon was "listened to attentively" by a full Senate.

"Nothing that has been spoken in the Senate from Oregon for years has received so much attention, here or elsewhere," the paper wrote.

The next day, Simon woke up "quite a famous man in the East, and especially in the anti-Quay papers in Pennsylvania," the Oregonian reported. A number of papers printed Simon's speech in its entirety.

The Philadelphia Inquirer, however, contended Simon ``proved to be an uninteresting talker'' and ``spoke in such a low tone that at times he could not be heard in the galleries.''

But Senator Carter was impressed.

After the debate, Carter ran into Simon in the Capitol and remarked, ``Simon, you owe me a bottle of wine for bringing you out as a Senate orator.''

Simon also drew praise from some other newspapers.

``Senator Joseph Simon of Oregon is a new man in the Senate, but judging from his speech on the Quay case he is manifestly very greatly superior to the average of the senators that come from the far western states,'' the Wilkes-Barre Record wrote.

The Philadelphia Record said Simon's speech struck a nerve with senators.

``If Mr. Quay should be admitted, asked Senator Simon, with great pertinence, what compensation could the Senate make to Mr. Corbett, who was rejected though he had by no means as weak a claim to the seat as that of Quay,'' the paper wrote. ``This is a question that appeals strongly to the equity and honorable feelings of senators.''

But the East Oregonian ridiculed Simon's speech.

``The people of Oregon will smile at Joe Simon's stand for `justice,''' the paper wrote. ``The fact is, he is the man who manipulated the Corbett deal, spent Corbett's money, and so dexterously played the game of politics that he put himself in the United States Senate.''

The angriest response to Simon's speech came, naturally, from former Senator Mitchell.

He called Simon a ``senatorial prevaricator.''

``Instead of discussing any one or more of the many important subjects now pending in the United States Senate.... the senator has signaled the inauguration of his national career of statesmanship by an unwarranted, unsupported and absolutely false, if not, indeed, malicious personal attack on me,'' Mitchell said.

In his response, in which he quoted Scripture and Shakespeare, Mitchell accused Simon of ``falsely professing'' to aid Corbett's candidacy while secretly working to bring about his own election.

``If Senator Simon and Senator Corbett and their associates—the

Populists in the Legislature of 1897—were of the opinion that my election to the Senate, for any reason, would have been a menace to the best interests of the state and the nation.... then why not have the honesty and manhood to say so?" Mitchell wrote.

He also attacked Simon's record as "pitted with acts of treachery" to the Republican party. Mitchell had his response printed into a pamphlet circulated throughout the state.

In Oregon, the Daily Journal of Salem sided with Simon over Mitchell.

"Simon is showing himself to be an independent man in the Senate," the paper wrote, calling him a man of "personal character."

The Washington Post noted, in perhaps an understatement, that the latest Simon-Mitchell tiff was "not likely to assist in bringing about harmony between the Oregon Republican factions."

Incredibly, a year after their public fight, the bitter enemies ended up Senate colleagues.

Mitchell returned to the Senate in 1901.

Simon, in keeping with Senate tradition, presented his fellow Oregon senator—and bitter enemy—to his colleagues, taking him by the arm to the front of the chamber to be sworn in.

Mitchell was given a "cordial reception by his colleagues on the floor, many of whom served in the Senate with him, and by his friends in the galleries, who greeted his appearance with hearty applause," the St. Joseph Gazette-Herald of Missouri reported.

Near the end of his term, Simon was reportedly asked to become involved in an investigation into whether importers were cheating the government out of custom duties by undervaluing imported goods.

The request was said to have come from J.R. Simon & Co., a New York-based silk importing firm owned by my great-grandfather Jacques R. Simon.

J.R. had come under investigation for allegedly undervaluing silk handkerchiefs imported from Japan in order to pay lower customs duties. The investigation made front-page news around the country. In the end, he was cleared of wrongdoing.

But J.R. believed one of his competitors was conspiring to defraud the government and tried to persuade the Theodore Roosevelt administration to investigate, "employing the influence of his relative, Senator Simon of Oregon," the Brooklyn Eagle reported in 1903.

There was no indication whether the senator got involved.

While Senator Simon was portrayed as anti-social, he attended social events, including a White House dinner hosted by McKinley for the Supreme Court and a tea party and piano concert at the White House put on by Edith Roosevelt. Simon also attended the Gridiron Club dinner staged by Washington's correspondents and Masonic events.

The senator also was reported to be taking banjo lessons.

"'Are you improving?' someone asked him," newspapers reported. "'Either that or the neighbors are getting more used to it,' he replied."

He could take a joke.

The Seattle Post-Intelligencer told a story of Simon receiving handshakes on the street, thinking it must have been for a clever mining deal he had engineered the day before.

But when one of his law partners congratulated him and asked, "Who's the girl?" he grew confused.

"'What girl?' stammered Mr. Simon,'" according to the article.

"Why, the one you are engaged to, of course,' returned the partner.'"

"Senator Simon's face turned an ashen hue, and he staggered back into his chair," the paper reported.

Simon headed to the records office and discovered that the groom was a banana hawker, also named Joseph Simon.

"The senator took the joke in a good-natured way, and later in the afternoon made it his business to meet the engaged couple and congratulate them," the Post-Intelligencer reported. He also planned to attend the wedding.

As Simon looked ahead to reelection, state lawmakers loyal to his long-time nemesis Mitchell passed a measure that would allow voters to express their preference for U.S. senator.

The thinking was that Simon, with the image of a political boss, "would not fare well in a popular vote and that his defeat would be more nearly assured than if it were left to the management of a Legislature—-where he was as nearly 'at home' as any man in Oregon," former Oregon Gov. Theodore Thurston Geer wrote in "Fifty Years in Oregon."

Compounding Simon's troubles, the influential Oregonian opposed his reelection.

Simon is ``not of sufficient force and weight to represent the state as it should be represented in the Senate,'' the paper wrote.

Never mind that the Oregonian, in earlier stories, had praised the senator for his attention to the state's interests and growing influence in Washington.

But now, the Oregonian declared Simon ``can do nothing for Oregon'' in the Senate.

``He has talents, but they are not the talents required for that position. The man doesn't fit the place; the place doesn't fit the man.''

The New Age newspaper, an African American newspaper in Portland, called the criticism of Simon unfair.

``He has not seen the press agent every day to get his name in the newspaper,'' the paper wrote. ``but he has quietly, intelligently, persistently gone about his duties, gradually making friends of the most influential Senators, working his way up on committees, gaining every month and week in influence.''

``He is not accused of any dishonesty, or trickery, or negligence, or inattention, or lack of interest in Oregon's affairs,'' the paper added. ``About the only criticism is that he isn't much of a speechmaker.''

When he does speak, the paper said, Simon could deliver a speech ``equal in true merit, force and influence to those of the more voluble senators.''

But other newspapers opposed Simon's reelection, harkening back to the way in which Simon won the Senate seat.

The Eugene Guard called Simon's election to the U.S. Senate an ``accident – at the close of a long, drawn-out session when members were not only tired out but disgusted with the muddle and voted almost without thought or care as to the result.''

"Did the public call Senator Simon to its service as senator of the United States from Oregon, or did he manipulate and scheme and work his way into that body?" the Oregonian wrote.

HIS CONSISTENT AND UNBLEMISHED RECORD.

Political cartoon decrying Simon's Senate record. The Oregonian, 1902.
Courtesy of the University of Oregon's Oregon Newspaper Project.

In 1902, Simon suffered a stinging defeat when his candidates for delegates to the county Republican convention were soundly defeated.

Simon's "Waterloo" was how one newspaper described the defeat.

Asked his reaction to the results, Simon issued a terse statement: "Senator Simon is very busy at this time, and does not care to talk."

But Simon did tell the Oregon Daily Journal that he felt he was treated unfairly by the Oregonian. The East Oregonian agreed, calling the Oregonian "the most potent influence" in bringing about Simon's defeat.

"I do not claim to have done very much in Washington, but I have done my duty," Simon told the Journal. "Many of the things I have done there have been credited to other members of Oregon's delegation."

A key factor in Simon's Waterloo was that Simon rival Mitchell and the influential Oregon editor Harvey W. Scott were "now friends whereas they have heretofore been anything but friendly," the Daily Capital Journal reported.

Simon's Republican allies explored forming a coalition with Democrats in an attempt to defeat the election of a Mitchell-backed Republican as Simon's successor in the U.S. Senate.

But the idea drew sharp criticism. The Pendleton East Oregonian warned that forming a coalition with Simon would place over Democrats "the hoodoo of a man who has just received the most thorough beating at the hands of his party that ever a man was given."

"It will be strange, indeed, if on election day Democrats who have so long complained of Mr. Simon's domination of our local and state politics should vote to re-establish him," the Oregonian wrote. "Should his 'Citizens" ticket be elected, he will expect to make it a basis for return to the Senate and for continuance of his control over the city and county."

In the face of likely defeat, Simon chose not to seek reelection, leaving the Senate when his term expired in March, 1903.

State legislators chose Charles W. Fulton, a Mitchell ally, to succeed Simon. When Fulton was sworn in, Simon watched from the back of the chamber.

In a 1904 story headlined "Downfall of a Dynasty," the Oregonian attributed Simon's fate to the way in which he was elected to the Senate in 1898.

"The circumstances of his election were such as to imbue many with the belief that treachery had been dealt somehow to the ostensible candidate, Mr. Corbett; and that to impress others with the conviction that if Mr. Simon had been as energetic in Mr. Corbett's interest as in his own behalf Mr. Corbett would have been elected," the paper wrote.

"It was hard to believe that members would be guided by Mr. Simon to vote for him, but could not be prevailed upon him to vote for Mr. Corbett."

Simon probably didn't mind leaving Washington. The Oregonian called Simon's Senate career a "bitter disappointment to him."

"Few men will leave the Senate with less regret than Joseph Simon," the Washington Post wrote. "He has not been fond of Senatorial life, and he has made very little effort to make the Senate like him."

Simon was like a "cat in a strange garret," the New York Sun opined. "He was treated with respect by other senators....but his own distant and even cold manner forbade advances."

"He seeks no admission into the circles through which things are accomplished," the Oregonian wrote. Newspapers called Simon aloof, saying: "He never seemed to be able to understand the spirit of the Senate."

Simon's role in denying Mitchell reelection to the Senate in the 1897 legislative hold-up made Simon "somewhat unpopular" among a number of senators, the Oregonian wrote.

Oregon's political boss also had difficulty adjusting to a lesser role in Washington.

In "The Most Exclusive Club: A History of the Modern United States Senate," Lewis L. Gould wrote about Simon's frustration in the Senate.

"'It is very difficult for a new senator to get very deep inside of the little ring that controls legislation in the Senate and, practically, the legislation of the country," Simon told a friend. "This little coterie of senators is extremely jealous of its power and will not permit an addition to its number."

"In the Oregon Legislature, he was a power, the most powerful man in the body," the Charlotte Observer noted. "In the United States Senate, he had no such power." The Senate had more powerful figures, including Sens. Nelson Aldrich of Rhode Island, Mark Hanna of Ohio, Thomas Platt of New York and Henry Cabot Lodge of Massachusetts.

Simon also became frustrated because of his weak influence with the administration, "nullified by those in his own party from his own state who opposed him," the Observer noted.

The Rural New-Yorker, a farm paper, suggested anti-Semitism contributed to Simon's difficulties in the Senate. "The race prejudice seemed to be strong in the Senate, and he was unable to accomplish much."

The final hours of Simon's Senate career were marked by a threatened hold-up, an irony given that Simon owed his election to the U.S. Senate to an earlier legislative hold-up.

Sen. Tillman of South Carolina (the same senator who engaged in a fistfight a year earlier) threatened to bring the Senate to a halt with a one-man filibuster unless Congress paid his state $47,000 it claimed it was owed for the War of 1812.

"The senator had a stack of books beside his desk almost as high as the desk, while on the desk reposed a volume of Byron's poems open at

`The Vision of Judgment'," according to newspaper accounts. Rep. Joseph Cannon, chairman of the House Appropriations Committee and future House speaker, denounced Tillman's demand as legislative blackmail. But lawmakers capitulated to Tillman as the cost of completing business.

After he left the Senate, Simon remained politically active.

In 1905, Simon joined the governors of California, Idaho, Oregon and Washington on a special train from Portland to Celilo on the Columbia River for driving of the last spike to dedicate the opening of a rail line he helped champion.

The Hood River Glacier trumpeted the opening of the railroad as "another epoch in the history of the commercial advancement of the great Northwest."

Perhaps more noteworthy was that Oregon Gov. George Chamberlain nabbed a diamond thief during the ceremony.

"A few minutes before the opening of the exercises at Celilo, the group of state officials standing on the flag-draped platform were startled by an exclamation from Gov. Chamberlain: 'That man's a thief!'" the Capital Journal reported. The thief attempted to steal a diamond pin from one of the dignitaries, but the governor caught the man.

For several years after Simon left Washington, friends urged him to run for the U.S. Senate again.

Simon was eager to vindicate himself of the earlier defeat, the Oregonian wrote.

But he declined to run amid concerns that his candidacy would revive Republican infighting.

"Simon Does Not Seek the Toga," read a 1907 Oregonian headline. "Thinks Old Wounds Would Better Be Allowed to Heal – Private Business Also Stands in the Way."

"He has a large political following throughout the state," the Oregonian wrote, "but is of the opinion that factional troubles might be renewed to some extent by his candidacy, and that they would better be allowed to heal."

Simon, meanwhile, remained busy with his law practice.

He took up a broad range of cases, from serving on the defense team for a prominent lawyer accused of murder (he was convicted) to fighting a speeding ticket issued to a local business executive (he won.). He even handled divorces.

Simon was involved in ``some of the most important and complicated litigations in Oregon's history of jurisprudence, in all of which he earned celebrity,'' the Morning Register of Eugene, Ore. wrote in 1898.

Simon and his law partner John Gearin defended Oregon congressman Binger Hermann in a nationally watched land fraud scandal.

The case was huge. The Oregonian called it ``one of the most colossal land frauds ever attempted against the federal government.''

High-ranking government officials, including Sen. Mitchell, the U.S. attorney for Oregon, both of the state's congressmen and a number of state legislators, were among more than 100 people indicted. Documents were forged, fictitious names were used and bribes were paid.

The case featured ``some of the best legal talent in the state,'' the Oregonian noted. A special prosecutor was appointed.

Hermann was indicted on charges of conspiring to defraud the government and destroying evidence by burning files during his stint as commissioner of the general land office.

Simon's representation of Hermann, a Mitchell ally, was surprising. As the Oregonian noted, Hermann ``trusted his interests and perhaps his liberty to the guidance and care of his old-time and bitter political enemy, Joseph Simon.''

Simon was one of the attorneys who defended Hermann in the fraud case, tried in Oregon. Hermann was tried in Washington, D.C. on the charges of destroying land records. Simon appeared as a character witness for him.

In 1907, Hermann was acquitted of the charge of destroying land records after a long trial. In 1910, a Portland jury deadlocked on the fraud charges, voting 11 to 1 for conviction. The charges against him were then dropped. By then, Simon had become mayor of Portland, and other attorneys were representing Hermann, including one of Simon's law partners, John Gearin.

Others, however, were convicted. Among them: Senator Mitchell.

It must have come as comfort to Simon, who attended some of Mitchell's trial, to read in the East Oregonian: ``Unlike leaders of the

Mitchell faction, Senator Simon has never been smirched by any suspicion of connection with the Oregon land frauds."

Mitchell, convicted of accepting bribes to expedite fraudulent claims, was sentenced to six months in jail, fined $1,000 and disbarred. He appealed the conviction. But while Mitchell was out on bail, the 70-year-old senator lapsed into a diabetic coma and died of complications from a tooth extraction before his appeal could be heard or the Senate could expel him.

Among Simon's clients was U. Simon, Sons & Cook, the San Francisco dry goods company founded by my great-great-grandfather Ulrich Simon. In the early 1890s, Joseph Simon helped Ulrich Simon collect debts.

Simon played a key role in a court case that led to the creation of Reed College in Portland.

He was among the attorneys who represented the estate of Amanda A. Reed in a case brought by heirs who contested her $1-million gift for founding of an educational institution in Portland in memory of her husband. Simeon Reed was an Oregon pioneer whom Simon knew well.

Another Simon client was Title Guarantee & Trust Co., accused of taking deposits knowing the bank to be insolvent.

His old nemesis, the Oregonian, took him to task for defending the bank.

``The affairs of the company ought to be administered in the interest of the creditors, not in the interest of the officials who plunged it into ruin," the paper wrote. ``Mr. Simon appeared in court a few days ago with an argument designed to protect the officials of the defunct confidence game from prosecution."

Simon in defense of the company argued that it was being charged under a recently enacted law that was ``not yet in force," according to the Oregonian. To which the paper wrote: ``But, senator, we know a statute on this subject, in an old law book, that is in force. It reads, `Thou shalt not steal."

Simon in 1911 was among a group of prominent Portland men who petitioned the governor to pardon the former bank president, J. Thorburn Ross. Simon also spoke at a hearing on behalf of Ross, a long-time friend and political ally.

In a high-profile case, Ross was convicted of misappropriating state funds on deposit at the Title Guarantee & Trust bank. Ross' supporters pointed out that the banker did not steal the money for his own use but used the state funds to pay the bank's general depositors when the institution failed. Ross was sentenced to five years in state prison. Incredibly, 11 of the 12 jurors who convicted Ross also signed a petition seeking the pardon.

``No one lost a cent,'' Simon told the governor, according to the Statesman Journal. Indeed, all of the school funds were paid back. Simon said that Ross may be guilty of technically violating the law, ``but I cannot believe he was guilty of any moral wrong.''

Ross got his pardon in 1913.

Simon also was among prominent men who sought to save a convicted murderer, J.M. Olberman, from the hangman's noose.

``Scaffold Was All Ready,'' read a headline in the Daily Capital Journal, when Gov. T.T. Geer, on the eve of the scheduled hanging, commuted Olberman's death sentence to life imprisonment.

Olberman shot his mining partner to death while the man was sleeping. Geer noted the victim threatened to kill Olberman, calling the dead man ``a bully by nature and a dangerous man.''

``Olberman committed a great crime,'' the governor said, ``but the provocation surrounding him makes him less guilty, in my judgment, than the other man who deliberately murders for either gain or revenge.''

It wasn't clear what prompted Simon to sign a petition on Olberman's behalf. But Olberman's plight drew widespread sympathy. The petition was also signed by the murdered man's daughters. In 1909, Gov. George Chamberlain, in one of last official acts, pardoned Olberman.

CHAPTER SIX
Taking on Teddy

Shortly after leaving Washington, Simon made national headlines by suggesting that President Theodore Roosevelt denied him federal appointments and worked against his return to the Senate because he was Jewish.

"Senator Simon Very Angry," read the St. Louis Republic headline. "Claims the President Discriminated Against Him."

When Roosevelt was governor of New York, Simon was a fan. He even urged T.R. to run for president.

"Senator Simon's words are among the very few indications that there would be serious talk of making me president," Gov. Roosevelt wrote to Portland attorney C.E.S. Wood in 1899, according to "Theodore Roosevelt: Letters and Speeches."

Simon got to know Roosevelt better when the then vice president presided over the Senate.

After Roosevelt became president, Simon met with him at the White House a number of times, including dining with him shortly after he became president.

After a while, Simon began complaining to the administration about unfair treatment in the distribution of patronage, a way for lawmakers to reward political supporters.

After leaving the Senate, Simon went public with his grievances.

He complained that he was the only Republican senator whose recommendations for federal appointments were "uniformly and contemptuously ignored" by the president. He contended Roosevelt also was "unfriendly" to his return to the Senate.

``I do not wish to believe that he entertains the view that one of my religious faith has no place in the Senate of the United States, that a Jew has no part in the government of this country; yet I cannot otherwise account for the treatment accorded me,'' Simon said of Roosevelt.

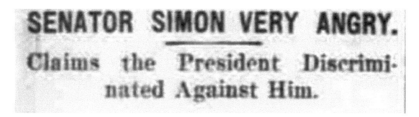

St. Louis Republic headline

The charges created a sensation.

``It is not often that a President has been directly charged with intentional falsehood,'' the Eugene Guard wrote.

``The spectacle of the chief magistrate of the nation engaging in a political controversy wherein his honor is one of the chief points of issue is sufficiently novel to attract the attention even of those who do not usually pay attention to such affairs,'' the Press Democrat of Santa Rosa, Calif. wrote.

Simon went public with his complaints after Roosevelt appointed a Mitchell ally over a Simon man as register of the Oregon City land office.

Simon produced a letter from Roosevelt promising to name George A. Steel, an Oregon Republican leader and long-time Simon friend, to the position. But the president appointed Alfred S. Dresser.

Further infuriating Simon was that the appointment came after Roosevelt tapped another Mitchell man, George W. Bibee, for a different Oregon post over Simon's objections.

Simon had earlier complained to Roosevelt about allowing Mitchell to ``practically dictate'' Oregon appointments, according to a Simon letter at the Theodore Roosevelt Digital Library at Dickinson State University. He also accused the president of making appointments without consulting or even notifying him.

Newspapers reported that Roosevelt gave Mitchell 16 appointments and Simon none, even though C.E.S. Wood, a Portland civic leader, wrote the president that Mitchell was ``less loyal'' and devoid of morals, according to Wood's letter at the Theodore Roosevelt Digital Library, Dickinson State University

Simon challenged the president to "show where he has ever accorded any other Republican senator the continuous insulting and invariable lack of recognition that he extended to me."

Roosevelt's promises, "at least those made to me, were, like piecrust, made to be broken," Simon said.

Simon complained that "many of my bitterest foes" have been appointed to federal positions, "in some instances as a reward for efforts made to prevent my return to the Senate."

Simon's charges drew headlines from Boston to Hawaii.

"Sore at the President," wrote the Minneapolis Journal. "Senator Simon of Oregon Says Roosevelt's Promises Are Like Piecrust."

"War Will be Waged by the Senator and the President," the Oregon Journal declared.

"No Love Felt for the Jews By Roosevelt. Statement of Simon Creates a Sensation," read a page one headline in the Atlanta Constitution.

The Oregonian said Simon "spoke of the alleged delinquencies of the chief executive with as much sarcasm as he might be expected to use in exposing the petty graft of a ward heeler."

Roosevelt was furious.

"Little Joe Enrages Roosevelt," read the headline in the Daily Journal in Salem.

Roosevelt did not directly respond to Simon's charges. But the president's allies dismissed Simon's charges as "mere yelp over political disappointments," the Los Angeles Times reported.

Roosevelt's record also seems to refute Simon's charges that the president was hostile toward Jews.

Roosevelt spoke out against the killing of Jews in Czarist Russia after Simon and other prominent Jews urged him to do so. Secretary of State John Hay wrote Simon telling him the president has "decided to accept your opinion, and that of other groups of intelligent American Jews whom you represent" and send a petition to the czar.

When Roosevelt won the Nobel Peace Prize, he donated a portion of the prize to the Jewish Welfare Board. Roosevelt also appointed the first Jewish Cabinet member: Oscar S. Straus as secretary of commerce and labor.

At a 1911 dinner hosted by the Union of American Hebrew Congregations in Roosevelt's honor, Jacob H. Schiff hailed the former president as "one, who more than any other American, living or dead, has taught the world the lesson that, equally with any other citizen of this country, the Jew is entitled to a square deal... We Jews owe him a debt of gratitude."

The administration attributed Simon's charges to the "startling state of infelicity" between Simon and Mitchell, as the Hutchinson News of Kansas put it.

Roosevelt, in a 1902 letter to Simon pledging to appoint Steel, expressed his frustration with the friction between the Oregon senators. "I do hope that on the next appointment you two can get together," the president wrote.

Simon critics contended the senator himself was to blame for his lack of influence with the administration. The administration believed that Simon "discredited" himself by backing Democrats over members of his own party, the Oregonian wrote.

"The President has the utmost contempt for a man who will, for personal advantage and out of personal spite, betray his own party," the paper wrote in reporting the White House response to Simon's charges.

Harvey W. Scott, the influential Oregonian editor, contributed to the White House's belief that Simon betrayed the Republican party. He wrote Roosevelt that the Simon machine was "thoroughly treacherous," working to elect a Democrat as Oregon governor in 1902, according to Scott's letter at the Theodore Roosevelt Center at Dickinson State University.

The Oregonian asserted that Simon and his allies helped Democrat George W. Chamberlain defeat Republican William J. Furnish because they wanted to keep a Mitchell ally out of the governor's office.

"In a Democratic governor, they have a man who is at least passively friendly to their interests," the paper wrote.

It was ironic that Simon, a Republican political boss, supported Chamberlain, a Democratic political reformer. But it was preferable than backing a Mitchell man, even if he was a fellow Republican. After

Mitchell died, Chamberlain appointed Democrat John Gearin, a Simon law partner, to fill the Senate seat.

As for Scott's attacks on Simon, it should be noted that the Oregonian editor harbored his own ambitions for a Senate seat.

Simon vehemently denied betraying the Republican party. The charge ``against my political integrity is without any foundation,'' he declared.

Simon said that he never uttered a single word against the Republican candidate for governor, contending that Furnish lost because he ran against a popular Democrat. The fact that the Republican candidate was previously a Democrat also dimmed GOP enthusiasm for him.

Newspapers attributed the election of a Democratic governor in solidly Republican Oregon to the divisions within the GOP.

The main reason for the Republican candidate's defeat, the Oregonian wrote, was the ``vengeance of a defeated faction'' (meaning Simon and his allies) and their ``lust for revenge.''

But the Seattle Post-Intelligencer said the Oregonian contributed to the factionalism.

``Maintaining a nominal Republican allegiance, it has defamed and defied the party whenever it desired to make men or unmake them,'' the paper wrote. ``Witness the unrelenting war upon Senator Simon, whom the Oregonian was largely instrumental in sending to the Senate.''

Criticism that Simon reached out to Democrats also was unfair, given that Mitchell also formed alliances with members of the opposing party. Mitchell relied on Democratic support to win back a U.S. Senate seat in 1901.

``Isn't it a well-known fact that the Simon faction was defeated by a combination of Mitchell Republicans and Democrats,'' the Polk County Observer asked.

Simon's attack on Roosevelt came a few months before the president embarked on a trip through the West, including Oregon, fomenting talk that the president might encounter Simon or at least face questions about Simon's charges.

``Suppose he and Simon should meet on the streets of Portland face-to-face?'' asked the Press Democrat of Santa Rosa, Calif. ``Will the `hero of San Juan Hill' lay aside his official dignity and proceed to have it out like they do on the plains of his beloved Wyoming, or will it continue as it has begun—a long-distance talking match?"

"Trying to Start Hebrew War Against Roosevelt," read a headline in New York's Daily Saratogian.

When Roosevelt visited Los Angeles, Rabbi Sigmund Hecht of Congregation B'nai B'rith alluded to Simon's charges. He called Roosevelt the "president of the whole people" whose actions are "not influenced either by political partisanship, or by religious prejudices."

Simon's defeat, the rabbi said, "was brought about neither by the interferences of the president, nor by religious prejudices."

Roosevelt, during a stop at Salem, Ore., appeared to have Simon's charges in mind when he declared that a "cornerstone in the building of this government must not be merely religious toleration before the law, but a genuine religious toleration among ourselves."

When Roosevelt got to Portland, there was no face-to-face confrontation.

"One of the first things the president did after being seated at last night's banquet in Portland was to send for Rabbi Wise, well known in New York, and he kept him by his side for more than half the evening," the New York Sun reported. Wise was Stephen S. Wise, formerly from Simon's Portland synagogue.

A New York Sun headline on Roosevelt's Portland visit read: "Hebrews Cheer Him in Spite of Simon's Crusade."

"The Hebrews had put up decorations with striking lavishness and cheered as loudly as any of their neighbors," the paper reported.

Simon was nowhere to be seen around Roosevelt during the president's visit.

But the Daily Record-Miner of Juneau, Alaska reported that Simon had been "flooded with telegrams from leaders of the Jewish race all over the United States, and many of them shower congratulations upon him for the stand he has taken."

Press reaction to Simon's charges was mixed.

Washington reporters said Simon's chilly relationship with Roosevelt was due to Simon's own coolness. They noted that Roosevelt often entertained Congressman Julius Kahn (R-San Francisco), a German Jewish immigrant, at the White House.

"If Mr. Roosevelt is an enemy of the Jews in public life, as the saturnine Simon suggests, he concealed his dislike cleverly in the case of Julius Kahn, with whom the president seldom failed to crack a joke and pass a jolly half-hour when the Californian called at the White House," the Chicago Post reported.

The Oregonian attacked Simon for "expending a lot of hot air uselessly," finding the ex-senator at fault for not doing more to ingratiate himself in Washington's ways.

"Senator Simon never took part in social life in Washington. He rather shunned it. He was not in attendance at any of the prominent social or official dinners; he never gave dinners to his colleagues or to people of social standing in the national capital," the paper wrote.

"Had Simon shown signs of sociability and a desire to mingle, there is little doubt that he would have been received with other senators."

In response to Simon's charge that Roosevelt broke his promise to appoint Steel to the lands office, the Oregonian wrote: "The president very properly holds that a promise such as he made to Simon was binding only during the senator's term."

The Oregonian also found fault with Simon for failing to pursue Steel's appointment more aggressively.

"Senators representing big states and senators of great prominence in the business and financial world, and who are reckoned as statesmen of the highest rank, do not hesitate to go day after day to see the chief executive about a small appointment, and it is these men that are most successful in 'shaking the plum tree' and securing appointments."

The Hillsboro, Ore. Independent needled Simon that his "last official act after a term gained without the sanction of the people and filled with disagreements with the administration was to call President Roosevelt a liar."

The Western Leader called Simon a "Lilliputian at Washington," who could only "watch in envy" while his colleague, Senator Mitchell, "plucked the plums of patronage from the federal tree."

The Arlington Record accused Simon of making the "meanest and most contemptible" charge against Roosevelt.

Simon "sulked and played the baby because he could not be the whole thing after Senator Mitchell was elected," the paper wrote.

Mitchell weighed in on the controversy, telling the Oregonian, "Nobody can gain anything by assailing the president."

But the Capital Journal in Salem, Ore., editorialized: "A man's word should be as good as his bond, even a President's."

In defense of Simon, the paper took Roosevelt to task for accusing Simon of misrepresenting the facts.

"Simon's worst enemy would hardly accuse him of twisting the facts for any purpose. He is noted for plain-speaking and truth-speaking," the paper wrote.

The Hillsboro, Ore. Argus, never a friend of Simon, lamented that Roosevelt's dealings with Simon show that a presidential word is "no more sacred than that of a precinct politician."

In 1904, as Roosevelt prepared to seek the Republican presidential nomination, Mitchell wrote the president urging him to prevent Simon from gaining control of the Multnomah County delegation to the national convention.

"If Simon should succeed in carrying the day at the primaries in Portland, Multnomah County, he will control the delegation to the next national convention, and he will control it against you," Mitchell warned Roosevelt, according to correspondence at the Theodore Roosevelt Center.

There was speculation that Simon might work for Roosevelt's defeat.

"Does President Roosevelt realize he has offended the most prominent Jew who has ever been in American politics and that on that account he may lose the entire Jewish vote of all the states in his race for reelection," the Oregon City Courier wrote.

The State newspaper in South Carolina noted Simon's charge of bad faith came from "one of the strongest representatives of the Hebrew race in America."

"If Mr. Simon can persuade any considerable number of voters throughout the land that he has been persecuted, as it were, by Roosevelt because of his Jewish blood, it will be a sad day for Teddy," the paper wrote.

Some newspapers placed Oregon in the doubtful column for Roosevelt because of Simon's charges.

Simon told the Oregonian, "I have no fight to make on Mr. Roosevelt," and "I know of no friend of mine who is opposed to his nomination." Even George Steel expressed support for Roosevelt's nomination.

"Oregon Is Safe. State Is In Roosevelt Column. Ex-Senator Simon Has No Fight To Make His Friends Will Work for the President's Nomination," read an Oregonian headline.

Simon noted that he had supported Roosevelt's nomination as vice president at the 1900 Republican national convention and was due to give one of the speeches seconding his nomination on his behalf but was unable to attend the convention due to other business.

Simon said he admired Roosevelt "because of his determination to uproot all corruption in public office," according to a story in the Medford Mail.

That appeared to put an end to the spat.

Two years later, just days after Mitchell's conviction in the Oregon land frauds trial, a prominent Portland businessman wrote a Roosevelt confidante expressing concern about the disarray within the state's Republican party.

"The old regime is ended, no new Joshua has appeared to lead the people, and Senator Simon is being importuned to resume the management by those Republicans throughout the state who have hitherto stood for decent politics," Addison Alexander "A.A." Lindsley wrote.

Raising the possibility of bringing back Simon to lead the party, Lindsley asked about Roosevelt's feelings about Simon.

"Has he forgiven him for the public expression of his resentment when he was denied any part of the federal patronage of this state? If he has not or is not inclined to do so, we are 'up against it hard' in Oregon for no other man now in sight who might be put forward can nearly equal Senator Simon's ability as a political leader and manager," according to the letter at the Theodore Roosevelt Center at Dickinson State University.

There didn't seem to be any lingering bitterness.

After Simon was elected mayor, he welcomed Roosevelt to Portland and was photographed alongside the president.

"Mayor Simon First to Grasp Hand of Rough Rider as Special Train Rolls Into the Union Depot," read the 1911 headline in the Oregon Daily Journal.

''When the ex-president caught sight of the mayor, his face lit in a smile, his teeth showing,'' the Morning Oregonian reported.

''Hello, Senator, I'm glad to see you,'' Roosevelt said. ''I said Senator, but I should have said Mr. Mayor, but I've been used to calling you Senator.''

Hizzoner welcomed Roosevelt to Portland, telling him the city had ''always been one of his warmest admirers,'' the Oregon Journal reported.

Simon joined Roosevelt and other dignitaries in an automobile as 150 Spanish-American war veterans marched through packed streets to shouts of ''Hurray for Teddy'' and ''Teddy in 1912!''

The mayor accompanied the president, an avid big game hunter, to a banquet at the Portland Commercial Club. The room was decorated like an African jungle ''where monkeys climbed in the branches and parrots and cockatoos screamed,'' according to the Portland Journal.

''The animals were stuffed,'' the Oregonian reported, ''but hidden criers with megaphones and other contrivances simulated the sounds they would have made if they had been alive.''

Mayor Joseph Simon with Theodore Roosevelt at 1911 Portland dinner. Courtesy of the Oregon Historical Society.

CHAPTER SEVEN
A job with ``more kind of hell" than Dante could imagine

Who would want a job described as the toughest in Oregon with ``more kind of hell in it than Dante ever imagined?"

Joe Simon did.

In 1909, he ran for mayor, notwithstanding Mayor Harry Lane's warnings about the infernal job.

``I shall not resort to the use of brass bands or anything spectacular in an effort to promote my election," Simon told the Oregonian.

He pledged a quiet and dignified campaign.

His critics had other plans.

Simon was brutally attacked by the Oregon Journal as the candidate of ``professional politicians, the corporations, the saloons and the heelers and job-chasers of the old machine."

Simon promised, if elected, to pursue a business-like administration ``without machine politics."

That pledge, predictably, drew ridicule from the Journal. The paper called Simon the ``chief engineer of one of the most perfect machines ever formed."

Simon committed to seek cleaner and well-lit streets, an abundant supply of pure water, and aggressively enforce the laws for the suppression of vice. He campaigned against the city's ``lavish" spending, ``excessive salaries" and ``unnecessary offices."

``I shall seek to bring about the abolition of useless offices and will resist to the utmost the creation of new offices that are not necessary for the public good, or that may add to the already heavy burden resting upon the taxpayers of the city," he vowed.

Simon portrayed himself as a reluctant candidate, agreeing to run only after the "repeated urgings by many of the best business and professional men of the city."

He easily won the Republican primary. He spent $75.75, "the cheapest price" a Republican candidate for Portland mayor ever spent to win his party's nomination, the East Oregonian reported.

Incredibly, the Oregonian, which savaged Senator Simon, embraced his mayoral bid.

"His knowledge of our municipal affairs is equal to that of any man, and in such affairs he has tact and judgment unsurpassed," the paper wrote.

Referring to Simon's reputation as a political boss, the paper wrote, "Times change, and men are changed with them."

"Like all men, as they grow older, Mr. Simon must turn away from the past, to the present and to the future. Men may say about him one thing or another. But it will never be asserted that he is not competent …or that he has used his political opportunity or official position for his own pecuniary profit."

The Journal, on the other hand, attacked him relentlessly.

"Simon Is Choice of Retail Liquor Men At Secret Meeting," screamed a front-page headline.

"Machine Politicians Rally to Simon," read another.

"Boss Rule, or Rule by the People – Which?" asked another headline.

The Journal, which backed former Judge Michael G. Munly, the Democratic candidate, reprinted criticisms leveled against Simon over the years by the Oregonian.

Simon's election, the paper warned, would put the interests of the railroads and his other corporate clients ahead of the public good. His candidacy represented an effort of "bossism to again fasten itself on the public affairs of Portland and Oregon," it added.

Simon, nonetheless, won election as Portland's 36th mayor.

He defeated four other candidates: a Democrat, an independent, a Socialist and a Prohibitionist to capture the $400-a-month job. He was 58.

Even after Simon won, the Journal remained hostile.

``It is impossible that Mr. Simon has been transformed within half a dozen years from a confirmed political boss and manipulator into a regenerated man of higher civic ideals, such as Portland should have at the head of her government," the paper wrote.

The low voter turnout showed a lack of enthusiasm for the new mayor, the paper sniffed.

The rival Oregonian noted, however, that Simon received more votes than the four other candidates combined.

While Simon's critics predicted his election would lead to a return to bossism, political reformers said it would not slow the momentum for their cause.

``Every substantial reform will abide; and neither Mr. Simon nor anyone else will ever be able to restore the old evil conditions, nor will he nor any intelligent person desire to do so," Thomas N. Strong, a Portland lawyer and vice president of the National Municipal League, told the Oregon Citizen.

Many of the city's ``high-minded men" supported Simon on grounds that ``things had changed from the old day and that whatever you say, Simon was never himself a grafter; that the city was badly in need of executive efficiency," said Clinton Rogers Woodruff, another member of the National Municipal League.

``Mr. Simon has made good," Woodruff said, assessing Simon's performance after a few months on the job. ``He has given assiduous attention to the duties of his office; and most of the departments of the administration are running smoothly, and with greatly increased efficiency."

Simon's election drew national attention.

``It is not often that a former senator enters municipal politics, but Simon, having been immersed in politics all his life, is not able to escape the fascination of running for office," the Washington Times noted.

Simon won because voters wanted ``judicious, quiet and efficient municipal government. There has been buncombe enough—and too much," the Oregonian wrote.

The Spectator newspaper called Simon's election a protest against Portland's previous ``fussy-wussy administration."

In keeping with his low-profile style, Simon took the oath of office in the city auditor's office "so quietly .... that scarcely anyone" in City Hall knew he was doing it, the Oregonian reported.

"No pyrotechnics—just a sane, business administration, is the gist of Mayor Simon's policy," the paper wrote on Simon's first day as the city's chief executive.

No smoking either. As mayor, Simon "let it be known at the City Hall that he will appreciate it if the officials having business there will kindly refrain from smoking," the Oregonian reported.

He became the city's chief executive during a period of rapid growth.

Portland was the nation's 28th most populous city with 207,214 residents, according to the 1910 census.

The city was still basking from the national attention it had received from staging the Lewis and Clark Centennial Exposition in 1905. Simon was among the incorporators of the exposition's corporation.

Automobiles were still a new phenomenon.

E. Henry Wemme brought the first automobile to Portland in 1899. In 1909, there were 552 automobiles registered in Portland, with Joe Simon among the automobile owners. (This was a decade before the state began requiring drivers' licenses.)

Flying machines were more of a novelty.

In 1910, an Oregon Journal headline declared: "Man Bird Amazes Thousands," a reference to the large turnout in Portland for "the first glimpse of the modern wonder—" a flying machine.

It wasn't clear whether Hizzoner attended what the Oregonian called the first opportunity for Portlanders to witness an airplane in flight. It wouldn't have been surprising if he was there, given that 35,000 spectators showed up. "The crowd was far greater than anybody had anticipated," the paper reported.

The "social evil" was a dominant issue during Simon's mayoralty.

Portland was no different than other cities around the country, engaged in an emotional debate over Prohibition.

During Simon's reign as mayor, leaders of the Anti-Saloon League, the Woman's Christian Temperance Union and other groups promoted their cause in Portland, including staging a massive "Oregon Dry" parade with banners such as "Sober Girls for Sober Men" in support of a 1910 ballot measure to make Oregon dry. (Before radio, TV and Twitter, an impressive parade was a good way to reach the masses.)

On the other side, famed attorney Clarence Darrow drew more than 1,000 people – with hundreds turned away – for a two-hour speech in Portland in opposition to the ballot measure.

The measure was defeated. But public opinion soon shifted, and Prohibition went into effect in Oregon in 1916, four years before it took effect nationwide.

Prohibition was such a dominant issue that the Western Hotel Men's Association, established to protect hotels against ``deadbeats and thieves," was now focused on the threat of Prohibition to the hotel business. ``The hotels cannot exist without the sale of liquor, and a city cannot exist without good hotels," a Portland hotel manager told the Oregonian.

Simon told the Oregonian that he would tolerate no gambling, no saloon openings on Sundays and no open and flagrant red-light district. He pledged to preserve good order and keep the morals of the municipality in good condition.

``One of the gravest problems confronting the new administration is the social evil," the Oregonian reported.

``I want a clean, moral city," Simon declared. (In spite of his pledges, Simon's critics pointed out that he was among prominent Portland businessmen who owned property used for gambling and other vice.)

Simon declared his intent to reduce the number of saloons in Portland, from 418 to 100.

``I never go into a saloon," the mayor told the Oregonian, ``but I do not favor the radical stand of the prohibitionist...While I do not need liquor myself, I do not feel like saying that no one else shall have it.'

Endorsing Simon's goal of cutting the number of saloons to 100, the East Oregonian wrote: ``One hundred saloons, properly conducted, should fully meet the legitimate demand for liquor in Portland."

Simon signed into law an ordinance imposing new regulations on the liquor industry, including freezing the number of saloons in the city ``until there is not more than one for every 1,000 inhabitants," according to the Oregonian.

In spite of his vows to crack down on saloons, Simon came under attack as having close ties to the liquor industry.

One reason was his opposition to Prohibition.

Simon contended that Prohibition was unenforceable.

Even before he became mayor, Simon drew the ire of Prohibitionists, sometimes unfairly.

Temperance advocates blamed Simon for Judge John B. Waldo's defeat for reelection to the Oregon Supreme Court in 1886 because Waldo was ``too much of a temperance man,'' as the Lebanon Press put it.

Simon "entered into a bargain" with the liquor industry to defeat Waldo, asserted "The Political Prohibitionist for 1888: A Handbook for the Aggressive Temperance People of the United States."

The Oregon City Courier called Simon's opposition to Waldo, a fellow Republican, ``an act of treachery.''

``The methods by which he defeated Judge Waldo for the supreme bench should forever damn him in the mind of every honest man," wrote the Corvallis Gazette-Times. The Statesman Journal said Simon would be a ``fit companion for the gentry that wear stripes in the little community east of Salem," a reference to the state prison.

Waldo was so furious with Simon that he refused to be photographed with him in a group picture following the closing of the 1889 legislative session.

``I won't have my picture alongside of Joe Simon's," Waldo told Oregon Gov. Theodore Thurston Geer, according to the former's governor's 1912 book ``Fifty Years in Oregon.''

Simon opposed Waldo's reelection, the Oregonian contended, because ``Waldo would not stoop to make a political boss' demands paramount to the honest opinion of an unbiased judge.''

``The object was to get rid of a judge who was not so complaisant to the purposes of Simon's combination of interests, political, legal and corporate," the Oregonian wrote.

Simon ``sacrificed the interests of the decent elements'' of the Republican party by ``deliberately `knifing''' Waldo and helping elect his Democratic opponent, ``a tool of the liquor men," asserted the Cyclopaedia of Temperance and Prohibition, published in 1891.

Simon, in a rare letter to the Oregonian, acknowledged that he opposed fellow Republican Waldo's reelection to the Supreme Court but rejected the criticism as ``unjust.''

"I dislike very much to enter in a newspaper controversy," he said, explaining that he made it clear during the Republican state convention that the judge's nomination was "distasteful to a large number of Republicans." (There was a belief that Waldo harbored anti-Semitic views.)

Simon was accused of distributing Republican tickets featuring the name of Waldo's Democratic opponent, Reuben Strahan, in place of Waldo's.

But Simon said, "There was no attempt on my part to deceive any voters."

Some newspapers, nonetheless, called for Simon's ouster as state Republican party chairman and even his expulsion from the party.

"Joseph should be retired, so that he can exercise his privileges exclusively as a private citizen," wrote the Statesman Journal.

"He is a traitor and a sneak, and is not a Republican," the paper added.

State Senator Simon again came in the crosshairs of Prohibitionists in 1887 when state lawmakers were considering placing a Prohibition measure before the voters.

The Lebanon Express newspaper predicted it would be kept off the ballot at the insistence of the "rum sellers headed by Joe Simon."

But the measure made it to the ballot – with Simon's support. It was defeated, however.

Still, Prohibitionists blamed Simon for the measure's defeat.

"It is charged that Joe Simon, chairman of the Republican State Committee, had charge of the liquor money-bags during the campaign, and he does not deny it," the Dodge City Times reported.

Simon later took on a legal battle on behalf of famed Oregon brewer Henry Weinhard, a fellow German immigrant.

Simon was among the attorneys who challenged a 1904 initiative that allowed voters to prohibit the sale of intoxicating liquors within their communities. The so-called local option law was upheld by the Oregon Supreme Court.

Ironically, when Simon became mayor, he advocated the local option.

"I think every community should have the right to say whether or not it wants any saloons," Simon said, declaring that there were too many saloons in Portland, according to a report in the Oregon Journal.

Mayor Simon refused to permit women temperance workers to enter saloons. He called the women's work worthwhile, but said, "I have never believed there is any good reason for a woman entering saloons," according to the Oregonian.

In addition to his efforts to reduce the number of saloons, Simon sought to close dance halls, regarded as another source of social evil.

He signed an "emergency" ordinance, "necessary for the immediate preservation of the public health, peace and safety," to prohibit anyone in a dance hall from engaging in any "immoral dance," including "The Turkey Trot," "Moonlight Waltz" and "The Rough Dance." Violators were subject to a maximum penalty of 10 days in jail and $200 fine.

"The 'moonlight glide' is waltzed with the lights turned low," the Oregonian reported.

Simon shut down a performance by entertainer Sophie Tucker at a Portland theater in response to a citizen's complaint that the famed singer committed an act "which grossly disturbed the public peace and grossly outraged public decency." The police chief attended the performance and said he saw nothing indecent.

But Lola G. Baldwin of the department of public safety for women pressed Simon to act and even brought copies of the songs sung by Tucker to the mayor.

Simon supported an ordinance that would empower the mayor to cancel any show on stage in a theater or in a moving picture house on the recommendation of a board of censors.

The idea of a board of censors grew out a complaint of "an immoral act" at a Portland vaudeville house involving "the singing of a certain song and by accompanying contortions," the Oregonian reported. An advisory censor board was formed in 1911. After Simon left the mayor's office, the city established the Board of Motion Picture Censors with enforcement powers.

Simon also sought to crack down on gambling in saloons but did not want to "interfere with the rights of individuals," telling the Oregon Journal, "If a man wants to play a little game of whist or poker in his own house, I think it will be best not to notice it. Or if members of a private club wish to indulge in a quiet game of chance, it will be no part of my policy to interfere." But he said he would crack down on clubs organized to conduct gambling.

There was mixed opinion on Simon's record in rooting out the ``social evil.''

Three months into his term as mayor, Simon was assailed by the president of the Municipal Association for failing to improve the moral conditions of the city.

Simon dismissed the association as a political organization that ``waged bitter warfare on me in the last campaign but which, since my election, has asked of me more favors than my most ardent supporter has asked,'' the Oregonian reported.

In 1911, when Simon ran for reelection, the Municipal Association again assailed Simon's record.

``.... bawdy houses, open gambling, white slavery, illegal liquor traffic, and all parasites and other evils attracted by the commercialization of vice, have flourished here,'' H.M. Esterly, secretary of the Portland Municipal Association, wrote the Oregon Daily Journal.

The Oregon Journal, a frequent Simon critic, said that as Simon was nearing the end of his mayoral term, the ``social outcasts'' of the city are probably more numerous than ever before.

``Throughout the Simon administration, the town was the rendezvous and asylum of roughnecks, and with an abandon not known before or since,'' the paper wrote.

Simon said there was only so much he could do.

``I have learned that the best of prevention and law enforcement cannot suppress the social evil entirely, nor will it be possible so long as the nature of men and women are as they are,'' he told the Oregon Journal in 1911.

Among the embarrassing episodes that occurred during the Simon administration, the city's police chief, A.M. Cox, was indicted for malfeasance in office for allegedly permitting ``disorderly houses'' to operate. Cox proclaimed his innocence but stepped down from his job after meeting with the mayor.

Hizzoner contended the indictment was ``not justified,'' declaring that the moral conditions of the city are ``better now than ever before in the history of the city,'' according to the Oregon Journal.

Less than a month after stepping down, the police chief was acquitted.

Simon was a tight-fisted mayor, declaring at the beginning of his term: "I am going to stop all extravagance. I believe the people want economy."

In rejecting a number of proposed bond measures, he declared that he wanted to make Portland famous "as the city with the least bonded indebtedness." He issued orders to city departments to cut spending.

He berated the park superintendent for buying two cougars at $100 apiece for the zoo.

When the park superintendent said he got the cougars at a bargain, the mayor snapped, "Oh, you believe in buying cougars just because they are cheap, do you?" the Oregon Journal reported.

In a 1912 article on municipal park band concerts, the Oregon Journal noted that Simon's successor allocated more money for concerts "because Mayor Rushlight is known to take a deeper interest in things musical than did his predecessor."

"'Whenever the question of park music came before him, (Simon) always maintained that all music sounded alike to him, and that personally he could do very well without any," the paper reported. During Simon's tenure, "the music appropriations were always pruned down to the very minimum in spite of requests from the public for more music."

He applied his tightfistedness to his own office, paying for his chauffeur and gasoline out of his own pocket.

Simon's penny-pinching drew criticism, especially his opposition to increasing the city's debt to buy parkland.

"If Mr. Simon were mayor of Timbuctoo, he would doubtless insist that the Sahara had enough oases," the Oregon Journal wrote. "The desert wanderer on the burning sands would have a different point of view."

Despite his resistance to buying parkland, Simon was credited with advancing a plan to build scenic Terwilliger Parkway "to show my friendly attitude toward the beautifying our already beautiful city," the Oregonian reported.

"A road of incomparable beauty" was how the Oregonian described the parkway, named after the family that donated land. When the first link of the parkway was dedicated in 1912, Simon's successor, Mayor

Rushlight, declared the boulevard to be "one of the city's most important projects," the Oregonian reported.

With the arrival of motor vehicles, Simon faced a new challenge that still bedevils big-city mayors: traffic congestion.

In 1910, Simon boasted, the city laid more hard-surface streets "than in all the history of the municipality."

Even so, thousands of commuters were "subjected to great annoyance and endless inconvenience" everyday due to opening of the drawbridges over the Willamette River during rush hour.

Simon sought to restrict the opening of draws during rush hour despite opposition from shipping interests. He took the matter all the way up to President Taft. In a victory for the mayor in the closing weeks of his administration, the War Department, which had jurisdiction over the bridges, agreed to extend the hours for closing of the drawbridges.

Simon supported a campaign by Portland mothers to restrict the speed of autos near schools to six miles an hour.

On another traffic issue, Simon signed into law an "emergency" ordinance prohibiting roller skating in the business district.

Another issue he faced: ensuring a safe milk supply.

At the time, half of the cows providing milk to the city were said to be infected with tuberculosis.

With Simon's backing, the city enacted a "pure milk" law requiring dairy inspections. "All dealers found to be selling bad product will be arrested and prosecuted with all the vigor and determination the city can command," the Oregonian reported.

A low point in the Simon administration came with the death of Fire Chief David Campbell, a friend of the mayor. Campbell died while responding to a fire and explosion at a Union Oil Co. waterfront plant.

At a tribute to the chief, the mayor's eyes were "dim with tears, and his voice trembled, for the mayor and chief had been fast friends for years," the Oregonian reported.

Simon responded to his friend's death by moving to remove dangerous oil facilities from the city limits.

Another hot issue Mayor Simon faced was prizefighting.

The Municipal Association traded punches with Simon over boxing matches, arguing that they were really outlawed prizefights and should be banned.

``I am determined that there shall be no prizefights in Portland while I am mayor,'' Simon said, the Oregonian reported. ``But I am not higher than the law and cannot stop boxing bouts....The law puts no ban upon these.''

Simon said that while he opposed professional boxing, he had no objections to amateur bouts.

During his time as mayor, Simon faced a tough decision – whether to allow the showing of a film of black heavyweight Jack Johnson's knockout of the ``Great White Hope'' James J. Jeffries in a 1910 boxing match billed as the ``fight of the century.''

Many governors and mayors around the country banned the showing of the fight film for fear it would ignite race riots.

Simon said he would permit the showing.

``I cannot see that the display of the pictures is any worse than the printing of the minute details of the fight in the newspapers.''

Yet, in early 1911, the mayor had a change of heart.

Portland police, on Simon's orders, prohibited a showing of the fight film.

The pictures were denounced as ``brutalizing and debauching, savoring of the lowest depths of hell'' at a meeting of the city's ministerial association, the Oregon Journal reported.

The mayor considered the fight a brutal spectacle, the Oregonian reported. The city sought to prevent the showing of the fight film under the ``nuisance statute,'' which prohibited any act that ``openly outrages the public decency or is injurious to public morals.''

In 1909, Simon remarked that he had never attended a boxing match, or ever planned to attend one, but noted that many others like boxing. He said he would allow a boxing exhibition, provided there be no betting.

During his mayoral administration, Simon dealt with an interesting criminal case: the poison tea mystery.

A package of poison tea was sent to Lola Baldwin, superintendent of the Portland Police Department women's protective division, and her friend, Mrs. Vaughn. It contained strychnine.

``The mayor has taken a keen interest in the detective work, and it was by his instruction that the contents of the package were subjected to microscopic examination and a chemical analysis," the Portland Telegram reported. "He has asserted that he desires no stone left unturned in the effort to bring to justice the person who would by so cowardly a method seek the lives of women who had incurred his animosity."

Mrs. Baldwin told authorities that Mrs. Vaughn's ex-husband had earlier threatened her.

Authorities arrested the ex-husband, C.C. Vaughn, noting that they had earlier suspected him of attempting to "blow his wife into eternity by placing a quantity of dynamite under their home," the Oregonian reported. Vaughn complained that Mrs. Baldwin "interfered with his domestic felicity."

Mayor Simon pushed for strict limits on unsightly billboards, a cause that drew support from ministers who objected to "indecent billboards" like those advertising "suggestive theater establishments."

"We have here the most beautiful city in the United States—some say in the world—and we cannot tolerate what tends to destroy its natural beauty," he said, according to the Oregonian. He supported a ban on billboards in residential neighborhoods, limits to the size of the signs in business districts and restrictions on "the character of advertising."

When he failed to win City Council approval for the billboard restrictions he sought, the mayor successfully led a petition campaign to put the issue before voters. It was an ironic twist to his political career, given that years earlier Simon worked against establishment of the initiative process.

When a billboard measure came up for a public vote, the industry fought it. Billboard company Foster & Kleiser took out an ad in the Oregon Journal asking voters: "Which looks the best to our visitors—a vacant, unkempt lot covered with weeds and rubbish, or a neat, businesslike, well-kept billboard?"

The measure, nonetheless, won voter approval.

Mayor Simon was less successful with another one of his causes— changing the system for funding the installation of water mains.

His proposal to shift the cost of water mains from property owners to water users led to cries of graft and pitted Simon against labor unions.

The proposal, critics argued, was a scheme by Simon and his friends to increase the value of undeveloped land they owned.

``The amendment proposed by Mayor Simon and his Special Privilege Friends would, if it had been approved by the voters, have taxed the cost of all water mains upon the people who use the water, instead of on the men who own the lots,'' W.G. Eggleston, a critic of the plan, wrote in the 1910 pamphlet ``People's Power & Public Taxation.''

When Simon and other city officials proposed the new system for financing water mains, ``they said nothing about having any personal or selfish interest'' in the measure, Eggleston wrote. ``If it had been approved by the people, it would have taxed nearly a million dollars out of the pockets of the water users of Portland into the pockets of Mayor Simon and some other officers of the city government of Portland.''

``I would not think of using my office as mayor to increase the value of any property that I own,'' Simon said, according to the Oregonian. He pointed out that he and his partners in a Portland housing development installed water mains at their own cost.

``No one need fear that the small consumer will be exploited to benefit the rich,'' he said.

Simon's proposal grew out of the lack of progress in laying water mains throughout the city under the existing financing system. ``There is no use in trying to lay water mains under the present law,'' Simon said, according to an Oregonian report. ``We have tried and tried to get bids for this work, but the contractors take little or no interest in it, owing to the doubt they have of collecting their money from the abutting property owners. It is a law that will not work.''

But opposition to Simon's proposal was so fierce that the mayor dropped the idea.

While Simon was attacked as cozy with Big Business, he took on Western Union, described as one of the most powerful corporations at the time, pressing the company to meet a city deadline to remove its unsightly poles and put its wires underground.

Simon drew the enmity of another group of businesses—theater owners—for his pursuit of regulation. He pushed for an ordinance that would require multiple exits at theaters, citing the devastating 1903 Iroquois Theater fire in Chicago where 600 people were killed.

``I made an investigation and found that in a large majority of the moving-picture theaters the only exit was that of the entrance to the building," he said, according to a report in the Oregonian.

The theater owners worked to defeat Simon's 1911 reelection because the mayor had the ``temerity to insist that the owners of these amusement houses should provide adequate exits for the protection of human life," the Oregonian reported.

Theater owners opposed to Simon's reelection went so far as to hire people to sit in the audience during shows and hiss when Simon's picture was displayed on screen.

Simon also angered fireworks merchants when he pushed for a law banning fireworks sales for Fourth of July celebrations, citing injuries and property damage.

``Mayor Being Besieged," read an Oregonian headline. ``Fireworks Merchants Fear Ruin if Sane Fourth Law Passes."

He pushed for construction of the Hawthorne Bridge, which opened in 1910 to the mayor's declaration: ``Let it open." The bridge, which originally served horse and street car traffic, is still in use. It is the oldest operating vertical-lift bridge in the United States, according to the National Register of Historic Places.

He also led a drive to build the Broadway Bridge over the Willamette River, overcoming a legal challenge and becoming the chief pitchman for sale of the bonds. He was among the first to buy bonds to finance the project.

The Oregonian said the project would be ``the greatest monument" of the Simon administration.

``The decision to build what would become the Broadway Bridge was fraught with political in-fighting, legal and financial delays, and numerous other complications," according to the application to the National Park Service which led to the bridge's placement on the National Register of Historic Places in 2012.

``All manner of obstructions" were thrown in the way of the bridge's construction, the Oregonian reported. But it said Simon ``never wavered" in his determination to complete the project.

The Broadway Bridge opened in 1913, after Simon left office. Simon did ride in a parade of more than 450 automobiles across the bridge at its opening, which was trumpeted by the Oregon Daily Journal as a "new epoch" in Portland's growth.

By 1922, the bridge was "so congested at rush periods that traffic over it is greatly delayed," the Oregon Journal wrote.

The bridge, originally painted black but now red, is still in use.

While the bridge was regarded by the Oregonian as Simon's greatest legacy, Simon himself singled out playgrounds built under his administration as his proudest achievement.

"I believe the playgrounds have been the best feature of my administration," he told the Journal. "I point to them with more pride than to any other civic movement."

He also was credited with taking on the "paving trust," opening the way for more competition – and lower prices to the city – for street work.

He pushed a plan to make Portland "one of the most brilliantly illuminated municipalities in America."

In the 1910 mayor's message, Simon reported adding 25 police officers to bring Portland's police department to 226 officers. He also reported that while the Police Department is "constantly in the public view and subject to frequent criticism from persons having selfish ends to promote, it is well organized, properly disciplined and effective." And crime was down, too, he reported.

During his mayoralty, the "first motor-driven apparatus" for the Fire Department arrived to replace horse-drawn equipment.

Mayor Simon and his fire commissioners tested the apparatus, reaching speeds up to 50 miles per hour. The 1911 display of the modern equipment proved "as good an attraction as a small-sized circus," the Oregonian reported, foreshadowing "the doom of the faithful old horse."

Among other things, Mayor Simon attended a 1909 commemoration of the 50th anniversary of the death of abolitionist John Brown, joining Salmon Brown, one of the abolitionist's sons who was a Portland resident.

He also presided over a "dress parade and review" of the 190 men of the Portland police force in "spotless uniforms," according to the Oregonian.

In 1909, Mayor Simon greeted President Taft on his visit to Portland and was the only Portland man to ride with the president in the automobile trip from the Union railroad depot to the Portland Hotel.

He urged businesses to give workers the day off to see the president, saying Taft's visit to Portland should be observed as a holiday.

Mayor Simon escorting President Taft during
Portland visit. Courtesy of The Oregonian.

After the presidential visit, the paving company Bitulithic featured a picture of the president and mayor sitting in a Peerless car in a newspaper ad for pavement ``fit for a president.''

Two years later, Simon received a White House invitation to attend the silver anniversary wedding celebration for President and Mrs. Taft but was unable to attend.

Mayor Simon, the gold-standard man, met William Jennings Bryant, the powerful champion of free silver, when he visited Portland in 1909. Simon described Bryant as ``America's most gifted orator.''

In 1910, Simon, to the delight of the women of Portland, led a drive to lower the steps on streetcars.

Women had complained the high steps posed a danger. They also sought to lower the steps ``so that a lady can ascend and descend without being subjected to the leers of male loiterers,'' the News-Review of Roseburg reported.

``Women Win Mayor,'' read a 1910 Morning Oregonian headline. ``Simon Finds Streetcar Step Too High for Comfort.''

``I usually walk to and from my home,'' the mayor said. But one day, he was running late and decided to board a streetcar. ``I took particular pains to note the height of the step and I must say that, in my judgment, it was too high,'' the Oregonian reported.

Simon wasn't much of a sports fan.

As mayor, he threw out the first ball at the 1910 opening day game for the Portland Braves in the Pacific Coast League.

``None of the 12,000 enthusiastic men, women and children who gathered to witness the great game of yesterday afternoon knew that when Mayor Simon walked out to the diamond, he pitched the first ball he ever had thrown in his life,'' the Oregonian reported. In fact, the game between the Portland Beavers and Oakland Oaks was only the second baseball game he ever saw. (In 1895, he attended a baseball game during a visit to Omaha.)

``I never threw a ball before in my life,'' the mayor said.

A year later, Mayor Simon hoisted the pennant for the Pacific Coast League champion Portland Beavers before about 10,000 fans at opening day of the 1911 season. Admission was 25 cents for the bleachers and 50 cents for the grandstand.

Hizzoner was a car enthusiast who bought a seven-passenger Peerless Touring car in 1909.

As mayor, he often used his car for inspection trips. He covered more territory on inspection trips than any four of his predecessors ``because he has a fast automobile in which to travel,'' the Oregonian reported. ``He receives a complaint about some street, a sewer, building or other object, and decided to see it for himself.'

Mayor Simon in his car, 1909. The Oregonian. Courtesy of
the University of Oregon's Oregon Newspaper Project.

Simon said he gained new insight of the billboard blight after traveling
around the city in his automobile to see the signs. Until he drove around,
"he never before realized so fully how obstructive they are and how
unsightly many of them are," the Oregonian reported.

No detail was too small for Mayor Simon.

He instructed the police chief to enforce a law "prohibiting
expectoration on the sidewalks or in public places," the Oregonian
reported. The action came in response to a request from the Visiting
Nurses Association for the city to enforce the law to prevent the spread
of disease.

He was asked to stop horses from stomping their feet at night and
keeping residents awake in a Portland neighborhood.

That was just one of the noise problems he faced. Mayor Simon also
was asked to keep newsboys from hawking papers loudly on Sunday
mornings.

Horse welfare also occupied Mayor Simon's time.

Hizzoner was asked to find ways to protect horses on slippery streets.

"The struggle of a horse in Portland is a pitiful one," the Oregonian
wrote in 1910. "Overloading, improper shoeing and working over hours
are the prevalent complaints. The slippery streets, necessarily so by

reason of the smooth surface paving, is making transportation almost impossible for the horses, especially on the grades."

When the Simon administration introduced motor-driven fire apparatus to Portland, the Humane Society cheered. "The time is coming when the use of horses for heavy draft work will be more the exception than the rule on the streets of Portland," Robert Tucker, president of the Oregon Humane Society, told the Oregonian.

The mayor also endorsed a law to ban wood stables after 188 horses perished in a Portland fire during his administration.

Simon in 1910 contributed toward the Humane Society's campaign to raise money for an "ambulance service for horses."

And, he enjoyed walking.

"One good trait of Mayor Simon is that he is much of a walker," wrote the often-adversarial Oregon Journal. "He is seen frequently moving about the city on foot. This is good for a man's health and temper."

Even then, politicians resorted to stunts to call attention to their causes.

Mayor Simon, believing that contractors' bids for city projects were too high, bid on laying of a water main – and won the $4,329 contract.

"I will advance the money for labor and material out of my own private purse," the Oregon Journal quoted him as saying. The mayor said he was determined to make contractors submit reasonable bids.

Another time, he grabbed a shovel to show dig ditchers the best way to lay a water main.

"The city's interests are watched over as never before," the Oregonian proclaimed in a 1910 editorial praising Mayor Simon.

"When has the administration of City of Portland been so energetic or efficient as of now?" the paper declared.

Among the more unusual jobs that came before Mayor Simon were letters he received from women asking for his help in finding them husbands.

"These letters seem to have been prompted by a letter sent out by some man in Oregon to the mayor of New York, in which it was said that there is a scarcity of women in Oregon," the Oregonian reported. News of the letter made its way into the Eastern newspapers.

The letters from women in search of husbands were just one of the odder incidents in Mayor Simon's life.

In 1911, a woman arrived at the mayor's office seeking to give a séance, according to an Oregonian story with the headline: ``Seeress Is Disappointed. Mayor Refuses to Receive Proof of Psychic Power.''

The woman, told that she could not practice clairvoyance in Portland, sought to show the mayor in his private office that she ``could peer into the future.''

``The mayor, however, was too busy to participate in the proposed séance,'' the paper reported.

Simon quietly performed many acts of kindness, the Oregonian reported.

The paper cited the case of a ``poor woman with children'' who asked the City Council for a free license to peddle pencils. It fell to Simon to break a tie vote.

``I am opposed to showing any special favors,'' the mayor said in voting to deny the free peddler's license.

``That was as far as the public ever heard of the affair,'' the Oregonian reported, ``but the fact is the mayor, immediately after the session, called up a friend over the telephone, explained the case to him, and asked him to go to the poor woman and arrange for her support until she could obtain means of earning a livelihood.''

``Had it remained for the mayor to have told, however, it would have been a secret forever.''

Simon also loaned out his car so that children could see what it was like to ride in an automobile or take a trip to the country.

``Many a time the mayor has sent his machine out all day with tired mothers and their children that they might have at least one opportunity of enjoying the pure air of the rural districts or of the parks, while he himself has walked or ridden in streetcars to keep appointments or make official inspections,'' the Oregonian wrote.

In 1910, Simon's name was floated as a possible candidate for governor.

But the Oregonian dismissed the idea.

``Mayor Simon has quite enough to do in Portland,'' the paper wrote. ``This city made a most fortunate choice in its mayor and would not willingly surrender him even to undertake the greater duties of the governorship."

The People's Press, of Portland, reported that if the nomination for governor were offered Simon without any division within the party, he might accept it. "His close and intimate friends say, however, that under no circumstances will he take it."

Yet, the Oregon Journal reported that Simon was "easily the most unpopular" of the prospective gubernatorial candidates outside of his political base of Multnomah County.

In the end, Simon declined to run for governor.

"I have troubles enough of my own as mayor of Portland," he told the Oregon Journal.

Near the end of his mayoral term, an Oregonian reporter spent a day with Mayor Simon highlighting the issues he faced.

"Nearly everyone knows him, so he scarcely ever reaches the City Hall before 9 o'clock, as he is frequently stopped on the way many times."

Simon was "beginning to mellow" as he neared the end of his mayoral term, MacColl wrote in "The Shaping of a City."

"He was the sole survivor of the old rough-and-ready school of Republican Party politics," MacColl wrote. "He no longer thrived on controversy. Compromise was preferable to litigation. Because he was now the grand old man of the state Republican Party, he assumed a sort of patriarch's role."

When he came up for reelection as mayor in 1911, Simon was reluctant to run. He declared that he "cannot afford to serve another term and leave my private business to suffer," the Oregonian wrote.

He agreed to run after "hundreds of busy men, who would not under ordinary circumstances, take the trouble and time to write a letter or to walk to the City Hall to impress their desires in person, have shown that they want no change in the head of the city government now," the Oregonian reported. The paper called it an "unprecedented demand on the part of the citizens of Portland for an independent candidate for mayor."

Scores of friends called, telegraphed and visited Simon at City Hall urging him to run. Supporters gathered nearly 5,000 signatures on petitions in less than three days. "I cannot resist the earnest and enthusiastic demand that has been made upon me that I stand for reelection," he said.

Incredibly, the one-time political boss campaigned as a reformer.

He ran with the support of the Oregonian.

The newspaper was unabashed in its cheerleading. Just as it had once filled its pages with harsh attacks on Boss Simon, the Oregonian sprinkled its pages with lofty praise of the mayor.

"Decency and good government are represented in the candidacy of Mayor Simon," the paper wrote in a news story, not an editorial.

"Throughout his long and active history in Oregon, Mr. Simon's personal integrity has not been impeached," the Oregonian wrote. "He has been above graft or the suspicion of graft."

"There is agreement that Mr. Simon is well-qualified and that he represents as mayor no one class of citizens as against the other," the paper added. "No one questions his probity or motives or genuine desire to give to the city the best there is in him for the city's good."

The Oregonian also reported that Simon's term was "by far the most prosperous and remarkable two years in the history of Portland."

The paper cited among his achievements: saving taxpayers "vast sums by reducing the cost of paving," and establishing children's playgrounds throughout the city and helping free the river of "scows and scow-dwellers" within the city limits.

A week before the election, the Oregonian featured a lengthy story quoting dozens of Portlanders expressing "deep appreciation for the work the mayor has done and for his great ability and probity."

"Graft,' a word never applied to him," read one comment.

Among the tributes: "fair minded," "a man of brains and experience," "a lawyer of great distinction and a businessman of great capacity and unquestioned probity," and "absolutely honest."

Simon championed a commission form of municipal government, a Progressive Era reform. He ran as the "independent-commission government candidate."

Simon said that under a commission form of government, "responsibility can be readily fixed and made apparent to the people."

His campaign ran a full-page ad portraying Simon as an opponent of the "'ward heelers' and all those interests which fatten upon the 'spoils' of the old city political system."

Another ad, pointing out Simon's support for the commission form of government, noted the commission form of government will "increase the efficiency of the governing body, increase the personal responsibility of officials, lessen the opportunities for graft, curb extravagance, eliminate petty politics...."

Simon's opponent, Allen G. Rushlight, accused Simon of "trying to deceive the people by pretending" to support government reform.

Simon was soundly defeated by Rushlight, a labor-backed Republican city councilman whom the mayor defeated two years earlier. Simon finished second in the five-man race.

"The Simon Machine Is Smashed," screamed the Capital Journal headline. The Roseburg Review called Simon's defeat the death of the Simon machine.

The Oregonian, in a front-page story on Rushlight's victory, declared Simon's defeat was the result of opposition from the liquor and brewery interests, the paving industry and "every other selfish interest inimical to the welfare of the city."

"Mayor Simon has always stood as an exponent of machine politics and as a friend of big business concerns. For him to run as an independent candidate and to make the race as one standing for reform looked like an absurdity," observed the East Oregonian.

"Simon Humiliated," read the headline in the Oregon Daily Journal.

"I have nothing to say," the paper quoted Simon as saying.

"Outside of feeling a certain tinge of humiliation at my defeat, I am not sorry that I was not returned to the mayoralty chair. I would not have continued in office longer than the first of the year, if I had been elected, as I would have given my strongest efforts to achieve the adoption of a commission form of government as soon as possible."

The Journal attributed Simon's defeat to his setting aside the will of the people by his earlier resistance to public docks. "That was an act that the people of Portland never forgave," the paper wrote. A mayor is "the servant, not the sovereign."

The paper also accused Simon of posing as a reformer. "His political past did not fit the part," the paper wrote.

The day after the election, Simon was back at his desk in City Hall early in the morning "as though nothing had happened," the Oregonian reported.

"He appeared to take his defeat easy," the paper wrote.

Simon told the paper he was surprised at the result "to a certain extent."

"I entered the campaign only at the urgent request of a very large number of leading citizens and consented to be an independent candidate only as a last resort, for the purpose of trying to save the city's business interests. I do not, therefore, regard my defeat as personal."

The commission form of government – a cause Simon championed – narrowly won voter approval in 1913.

Under Portland's unusual commission form of government, the mayor and four elected commissioners make up the city council, who perform legislative and executive duties, including managing city departments. A city auditor also is elected.

On July 1, 1911, Simon welcomed his successor to the mayor's office. The Oregonian called it the first time in city history that an outgoing mayor was on hand to greet his successor.

"I can sincerely say that I found a good deal of pleasure in serving the public," Simon said on leaving the mayor's office, according to the Oregonian.

He was moved to tears when members of his executive board surprised him with a tribute and presented him with a silver loving cup, the Oregonian reported.

The Oregonian praised Simon's "notable record of achievement."

"He has given two years of the most painstaking and conscientious service to the public," the paper wrote. "He has worked all the time at the job."

Simon remained politically active after his defeat.

Though a teetotaler, he pushed a ballot initiative to promote the state's beer industry, serving on the "Equal Rights to Oregon Industry" Committee. (Even then, proponents of ballot measures came up with appealing names for their causes).

The 1916 initiative sought to lift a state ban on the manufacture of beer within the state. Its members ranged from Simon, the consummate political insider, to U'Ren, the political reformer.

Proponents sought to portray the initiative as an economic measure designed to boost an important Oregon industry rather than an effort to promote drinking. They also argued that they were seeking ``fair play'' by giving Oregon brewers the same rights as out-of-state brewers.

Among the more novel arguments in support of the measure was that it would promote ``true temperance'' by permitting low-alcohol beer as opposed to an ``intoxicating liquor.'' Additionally, proponents pointed out, alcohol-heavy patent medicines were already widely available.

``Conscientious physicians of the highest standing are prescribing beer for nursing mothers and for building up tissues in weak bodies,'' said one of the pro-arguments in the voters' guide.

``A law which permits the consumption of strong liquor brought into the state from outside yet discriminates against even a light beer made in Oregon from Oregon barley and hops is neither logical nor just,'' said the argument in support of the measure.

Proponents of the beer amendment even quoted Thomas Jefferson: ``No nation is drunken where wine is cheap.''

The measure was defeated, however.

Even after he left public office, Simon remained committed to Oregon's economic growth.

In 1913, he joined a group of prominent Oregonians to push for improvements to the Columbia River to ensure that the river would become what the group called ``one of the really great waterways of the world for the interchange of traffic between railroads and ocean vessels.''

Simon was involved in charitable work, including putting down the first $1,000 toward building of an old people's home for German Americans in Portland. He also contributed to the Portland Art Museum and the Hebrew Sheltering and Immigrant Aid Society.

Simon was a trustee of the Portland Woman's Union, which provided housing for young "self-supporting" women. He was a president of the Lang Syne Society, an organization of pioneer Portland businessmen. And, he was a member of the Chamber of Commerce, Oregon Historical Society, Oregon Pioneer Association, and the Concordia Club, a Jewish social club.

Simon was involved in humanitarian work, including helping to lead Portland efforts to aid Jews persecuted in czarist Russia.

He was a member of a committee that worked to provide relief to starving Belgians suffering from the ravages of World War I. The committee worked with a commission headed by future president Herbert Hoover.

As war raged in Europe, Simon supported the American Field Service, a volunteer ambulance service.

In 1915, Simon was among 100 prominent Oregon signers of a petition sent to President Woodrow Wilson urging him to use the influence of the United States to bring about ``a speedy conclusion of existing hostilities" in Europe. Just weeks later, however, a German U-boat sunk the passenger ship Lusitania, killing about 1,200 people, including more than 120 Americans.

After the United States entered the Great War, Simon served as a Portland leader of the Jewish Welfare Board, established to maintain ``the good cheer and buoyant spirits" of American Expeditionary Forces in France.

The board tended to the spiritual needs of Jewish soldiers, including sending matzos overseas for Passover. But it also provided recreation to soldiers of all faiths, including furnishing cigarettes and staging vaudeville shows. After the war ended, the board assisted soldiers in returning to civilian life, including offering classes in bookkeeping and farming.

In 1917, Simon was among the organizers of an Oregon branch of the League to Enforce Peace.

The national group, headed by former President William Howard Taft, advocated an international organization akin to President Woodrow Wilson's League of Nations.

Simon's support of the group put him at odds, once again, with Theodore Roosevelt.

The hawkish Roosevelt dismissed league members as ``apostles of feeble folly," accusing the league of opposing preparedness and advocating disarmament. Taft disputed Roosevelt's representation of the league.

The league said it was not a peace-at-any-price movement. It supported the creation of a world court to settle international disputes and the use of economic sanctions and military force against a member nation that goes to war against another without first seeking arbitration.

Simon also aided the war effort by buying Liberty Bonds.

After the war ended, Simon was named by the Portland mayor to help plan the city's Armistice Day celebration.

In 1919, Simon served on a panel that planned President Woodrow Wilson's visit to Portland. As mayor, Simon in 1911 met Wilson, then governor of New Jersey.

Wilson's visit to Portland was part of a cross-country tour to promote the League of Nations, an idea that enjoyed strong support from Oregon Republicans and Democrats alike.

So enthusiastic were Portlanders that more than 30,000 people participated in a lottery for 7,000 tickets to Wilson's speech.

Only a few weeks later, Wilson suffered a severe stroke.

In 1922, on the 50th anniversary of his legal career, Simon was honored at a banquet at the Portland Hotel attended by 250 fellow lawyers.

``Joseph Simon's word is his bond,'' said Judge Henry E. McGinn, according to the Oregonian account. ``He is an example and an object lesson to young men—an example of what diligence and work can accomplish.''

When Simon turned 75, the Oregonian asked him about his life.

``'I am an optimist and have lived a pretty conservative life,'' he said. ``I have been moderate in my ways of living.... I have cultivated steady habits....I go to bed moderately early, sleep well, and arise moderately early. I am a light eater and I walk to and from my home daily.''

At age 80, he told the Oregonian that he was enjoying contract bridge and listening to the radio. And, he was still practicing law, walking to the office and putting in a full day's work.

Simon died Feb. 14, 1935 of pneumonia at age 84.

His death, the Capital Journal noted, removed ``the last of the political bosses who dominated politics in Oregon.''

A few weeks after his death, the Portland City Council paid tribute to its ``lovable citizen.'' Oregon's governor, Portland's mayor and judges were among the dignitaries who attended his memorial service.

Simon is buried at Portland's Beth Israel Cemetery.

While the ``most notorious boss Oregon has ever known'' is little remembered today, reminders of his decades of public service can be found in the bridges, parks, and other civic improvements he championed in his beloved Portland.

Political reforms spurred by Simon and other political boss' wheeling and dealing—like the widely used initiative—also endure.

So, whenever you step into a voting booth, remember Joe.